IF YOU OWN A PRESERVE —

IF YOU PLAN TO START ONE —

OR IF YOU JUST WANT TO HELP

GAME BIRDS THRIVE

. . . here's a valuable guide on managing land areas to meet Game Bird requirements, selecting stock, breeding, feeding and rearing.

This common-sense book supplies the basic information you need to raise game birds in captivity or in open areas.

Raising
Game Birds

An authoritative, practical guide to producing pheasants, quail, grouse, chukars, ducks, geese and other game birds for pleasure and profit.

By Dan W. Scheid

Lessiter Publications

For more than 20 years, readers have trusted us to
deliver the latest information through our magazines,
newsletters, books, reports and conferences.

With knowledge being your most important tool,
Lessiter Publications provides valuable ideas to help you
exceed your goals and expectations. Our role is to treat you
as we like to be treated, offering quality service and products
that establish us as a leader in the fields we serve.

For information on other books or publications offered
by Lessiter Publications or to receive a free catalog, write to:

**Lessiter Publications, Inc.,
P.O. Box 624, Brookfield, WI 53008-0624.**

Or contact us at:

Telephone: (800) 645-8455 (US Only) or (262) 782-4480
Fax: (262) 782-1252 • **E-Mail:** info@lesspub.com
Web site: www.lesspub.com

CONTENTS

Pictorial Credits

Felix Summers of the United States Department of Agriculture, Soil Conservation Service, pages 9, 10, 13, 17, 19, 21, 22, 23, 25, 32, 50, 82, 84, 91.

Scruggs Quail Feeders Co., page 40.

Wisconsin Conservation Department, pages 50, 51.

University of Wisconsin, page 104.

Wildlife Management Institute, page 35.

The Highsmith Co., Inc., pages 48, 56, 66.

FOREWORD

More and more people are considering game birds a valuable enterprise. When properly managed, they can be produced and harvested much like any other crop. Often, under the right conditions, they can also serve as a secondary by-product of the land.

There are three fields of game bird ranching that offer excellent business opportunities to people who wish to spend all or part of their time working with pheasants, quail, chukars, mallard ducks, or other game birds. They are:

1. *Raising game birds for specialty meat purposes.* As the American standard of living climbs, people demand more delicacies on their tables. The average housewife now can afford to buy game birds when her market place can supply them.

2. *Raising birds to supply or maintain private shooting preserves.* Such areas are opening all over the country. Many of them would like to work with a reliable supplier who can furnish rugged, strong-flying, well-feathered birds.

3. *Keeping breeders to sell eggs and chicks.* Many people today are raising game birds to supply their own table or to give or sell to friends. They buy chicks and eggs from breeders, hatcheries, farm supply stores, and feed dealers. Many people raise fancy game birds as a hobby.

It is unfortunate but with intensive farming and the increasing sprawl of our cities, wild game birds in many areas no longer can thrive unaided. They need a helping hand—that of an individual who has learned the basic facts of propagation and applies them to the species he wishes to see thrive.

Raising game birds is done under two types of conditions—in large open areas or in captivity. Both serve their purpose and shall be considered in this book.

Raising game birds in captivity is a relatively new idea that has developed rapidly over the past twenty-five to thirty years. It offers a real challenge to those persons who like to work outdoors close to nature.

The purpose of the following chapters is to supply most of the basic knowledge necessary for raising game birds under both environments—in captivity and/or in open areas. It cannot, of course, be a "primer" for all details but will give the necessary knowledge which when added to "common sense" should make it possible to successfully raise game birds of certain adapted species.

Chapter I

PROPAGATING GAME BIRDS IN OPEN AREAS

Generally speaking, game birds are quite prolific and their requirements for existence are few and can be easily provided. Briefly these requirements are: food, cover, protection from natural enemies, and an adequate environment. If any one of these essentials is lacking, there is little chance for successful propagation.

As with any crop raised, certain things must be done or provided before success in raising game birds can be achieved. Whether or not you are successful will depend upon:

1. Size and type of land area available.

2. Use now being made of the land.

3. Kind of game birds that are propagated.

4. Management practices you perform with the area and the birds.

The factors which control wildlife populations can be divided into biotic agencies, physical agencies, and those of the habitat. Under the biotic agencies are predators, diseases and parasites. Man's activities and weather conditions are classified as physical agencies. Water, cover, and food are each part of a desirable habitat. These factors are shown in the following illustration:

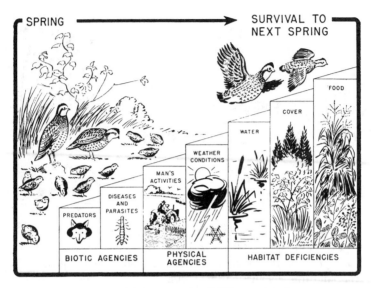

Factors which control wildlife population.

Actually, only a few of these factors can be entirely controlled by man. The effects of predators may be modified, but often with uncertain results. Little can be done about common diseases and parasites, except perhaps at the rearing stages. Some of man's activities, such as the management of the land, could be changed. The greatest changes, fortunately, can be made in the more important factors. Generally speaking, success in managing land to produce useful game birds lies in improving the amount, quality, and distribution of food, cover and water.

At this point, one would reason that the best way to control these essential factors would be to raise all game birds in captivity. However, this is not necessarily the case. Requirements of raising game birds in open areas will be considered first. This, in reality, is the natural way and the information given will help also in raising birds in captivity.

Game Bird Requirements In Open Areas

While no two kinds of wildlife have exactly the same requirements for living, as stated earlier, it is safe to say that all kinds need food, cover, water, and an adequate environment.

To support a high game bird population, the area must have a plentiful supply of food close to cover that furnishes protection from enemies and weather. Also, it must be available in all seasons of the year.

In most land areas of the United States, there is enough food from late spring to fall—insects, wild fruits, weed seeds, waste grain, nuts, or green plants. The critical season is winter, though early spring is often just as critical. From December through March, there are very few insects, many wild fruits are gone, and snow and ice may cover other food. In the South, planting good food close to cover is the best way to be sure you have enough game bird food throughout the year. In the North, you can extend cover plantings close to natural sources of important foods or leave unharvested a part of the grain crop close to good cover.

Most kinds of game birds need several kinds of cover. Cover must conceal nests and young and provide shade from the hot sun and shelter from chilling rains. It must allow escape from enemies and it must protect against snow, sleet, cold, and wind in winter. There are three essentials to good cover for game birds—grass, weeds, stubble, and other low-growing plants for nesting and roosting; dense or thorny shrubs for protection from predators, loafing, and nesting; and in the North, clumps of evergreens or other tall dense cover for winter protection. All three kinds of cover should be close together and near food.

Game birds can get water from surface water, food, and dew. In the East and South, upland game birds can survive on succulent foods and dew. Surface water is a necessity for most kinds of game birds in the more arid West, as it is everywhere for water-loving species like ducks and geese.

Managing Open Land Areas
To Meet Game Bird Requirements

If there is adequate land on a farm, ranch, or in your "rurban" area, raising game birds is a crop that can be enjoyed by the land owner and his family and friends; it is a secondary harvest from which he doesn't expect an income. On some farms and ranches it is one of several important crops. The land owner devotes a portion of his land to game birds; that is, he modifies his management of fields in other crops so as to encourage game. But on other farms and on many "rurban" homesites, raising game birds is the primary crop; management is aimed at producing maximum bird yields.

Many common farm practices are helpful to wildlife, others are harmful. Following are some of both practices summarized by the United States Department of Agriculture.

Cropland practices **helpful** to game birds are:
1. Cropping systems that include grass-legume meadows.
2. Liming and fertilizing.
3. Stripcropping.
4. Cover crops.
5. Stubble-mulch tillage.
6. Delaying mowing of headlands, roadsides, and watercourses until after the nesting season.
7. Leaving unharvested $\frac{1}{8}$ to $\frac{1}{4}$ acre of grain next to good cover.

Practices **harmful** to game birds on cropland include clean fall plowing; mowing of watercourses and headlands before ground-nesting birds have hatched; and burning of ditchbanks, fence rows, and crop residues.

Pastureland practices **helpful** to game birds include:
1. Grazing within the carrying capacity of the pasture.
2. Liming and fertilizing.
3. Reseeding, renovating, or over-seeding with legumes.
4. Building ponds for livestock water.
Pastureland practices that are **harmful** to game birds are uncontrolled burning, overgrazing, and completely clean mowing early in the season.

Rangeland practices **helpful** to game birds include:
1. Proper grazing and salting.
2. Watering places for livestock.
3. Reseeding.
4. Construction of walkways in marshy range.
5. Partial brush removal.
Practices that are **harmful** to game birds on rangeland are overgrazing and complete brush removal.

LET WILDLIFE IN FENCEROWS WORK FOR YOU

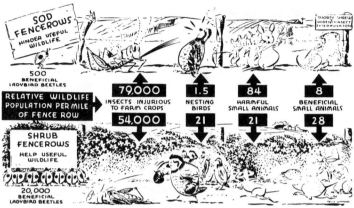

·LET SHRUBS GROW IN YOUR FENCEROWS · CUT OUT TREES AND VINES · PLANT LIVING FENCES OF MULTIFLORA ROSE

Woodland practices that are **helpful** to game birds include:

1. Protection from unwanted fire and harmful grazing.
2. Selective cutting in small woodlands.
3. Piling brush near the edge of the woods.
4. "Release" cuttings to increase production of acorns, nuts, and other tree seeds useful for game food.
5. Cutting trees out of woodland borders to increase the growth of shrubs for food and cover.
6. Seeding clovers and grasses along roads and trails and in woodland openings.

Woodland practices **harmful** to game birds are uncontrolled burning and grazing.

Land for game birds includes any land managed especially to produce desired species. Many of the helpful practices listed above under other land uses are also applicable to game bird land.

Special practices include:

1. Controlled burning.
2. Food-patch planting.
3. Mowing or using herbicides to keep woody plants out of areas that should stay in low-growing grasses, legumes, and other herbaceous plants.
4. Seeding grasses and legumes.

5. Planting trees and shrubs, especially in prairie areas.

6. Managing water—this includes construction of earth fills, installation of water-level control structures, and, in the arid parts of the country, establishing watering places.

There are eight kinds of areas that can be managed especially for game birds. Namely, they are wetlands, ditchbanks, odd land areas, ponds, fence rows and hedges, borders, windbreaks, and streambanks. Recommendations for the treatment of each area follows.

Use of Wetlands

Many wet areas throughout the United States can be improved to produce ducks and other kinds of game birds that like to live near or in water.

Generally, it is recommended that you manage marshes either for fur-bearing mammals or for waterfowl. If managed for one they tend to be somewhat useful for the other, but you cannot have best conditions for both on the same area. For either purpose, three requirements must be met: (1) A dependable water supply, (2) water-level control, and (3) the right kinds and amount of vegetation for feeding, nesting, and resting.

For small marshes, the simplest management is careful control of livestock grazing and of burning. Too much grazing destroys valuable food and cover. Some marshes should be protected from all grazing until after choice duck-food plants have matured. Burning can be important in marsh management, but only when done correctly. You should get technical advice on when, where, and how to burn your marsh.

Many wetlands are so overgrown with marsh plants that there are no areas of open water. Such wetlands can be greatly improved for ducks by removing vegetation in strips 30 to 50 feet wide. Methods of removing undesired vegetation include spraying with herbicides or using dynamite or a dragline. Temporary clearings can be made by mowing when the marsh is dry or by blading on the ice.

The importance of loafing spots to waterfowl is generally not fully appreciated. Small islands, knolls, sandbars, open margins, or exposed mudflats are valuable for this purpose. Firmly anchored floating logs or rafts are used by ducks as loafing, sunning, sleeping, and preening spots. Rock piles and old bales of hay or straw in the shallower parts of a marsh will serve the same purpose.

Marshes in duck-nesting areas should have six or more inches of water for at least three months in spring and early summer. If your marsh does not, you can improve it for ducks and other waterfowl by digging or blasting one or more holes about thirty feet in diameter and two to three feet deep.

A marsh area larger than five acres with a reliable water supply from a stream, spring, or reservoir may be improved for game birds by controlling the water level. You will need engineering help to find out if a water-level-control structure is allowed and can be built at a feasible cost.

To manage a marsh for waterfowl by controlling the water levels, you have two choices. One method is to draw the water down enough to keep the soil moist—but with no water on the surface—during the growing season. This will favor growth of smartweed, burrweed, wild millet, and other good waterfowl plants.

In the fall the area should be flooded to a depth of 1 to 15 inches to make it attractive to ducks. This method produces the most duck food but it does not provide nesting for waterfowl.

The other method is to maintain the water level at depths between 15 and 30 inches throughout the season, holding it at 15 inches in the fall. This method will favor the growth of waterfowl-food plants such as wild celery, sago and other pondweeds, arrowhead, naiads, duckweed, and stonewort. These are fair to good duck foods.

If you have a marsh larger than 5 acres that does not have reliable surface water but that does have a water table that keeps water within 1 foot of the surface, you may be able to improve it for raising ducks with level ditches. You will need help from your local soil conservationist to find out if your marsh has soil suitable for ditching and to determine the best arrangement for the ditches.

Many land areas have fields that can be planted to choice duck foods, cultivated, and later flooded so the ducks can readily eat these foods. Such fields are much more attractive to ducks than fields of the same crops grown on dry land that cannot be flooded.

The best foods to grow in duck fields are corn, browntopmillet, smartweed, barnyardgrass, Japanese millet, and buckwheat. For duck use, these crops must be flooded to depths of 1 to 15 inches with water previously stored in a nearby pond, reservoir, or flood-control structure. Water might also come from a stream, irrigation canal, bayou, or well. It can be brought to your duck field by gravity flow or by pumping. In most parts of the country, except perhaps coastal Oregon and Washington, you can't depend on runoff water from fall rains for this flooding.

For a good duck field, you must be able to control the water. For spring or summer cultivation you will need some way to drain off the water. During fall and winter a control structure to regulate the water depth is necessary. Ask your local soil conservationist for help in selecting sites and planning needed structures or other devices.

Coastal marshes require special consideration because of the possibility of changing the salinity of the water and its effects on vegetation. Be sure to get help from a soil conservationist before attempting ditches or controlled water levels on coastal land.

Management Of Ditchbanks For Game Birds

Water is usually present in drainage and irrigation ditches during the spring and summer. Game bird food is often available in nearby crop fields. Cover added in the form of grasses and legumes makes ditchbanks ideal places for wild birds to live. It also protects the ditch and prolongs its usefulness.

Ditches filled with willows, cottonwoods, or other trees and shrubs are not able to carry the flow of water they were designed to handle. They provide poor drainage for land that might otherwise produce good crops.

Your first aim in good ditchbank management should be to establish and keep grass on the banks. Use grasses that offer real competition to the woody plants that would otherwise invade the ditch and lower its water-carrying capacity.

This treatment also makes cleanout and maintenance easy.

STREAMBANK IMPROVEMENT

Seeding grasses on the subsoil of steep ditchbanks is often difficult. Your local soil conservationist can advise you on soil treatments, kinds of grasses to seed, and seeding methods. He can also tell you what legumes to mix with the grass.

In many places strong winds may blow soil from adjoining tilled fields. This soil is dropped in the bottom of ditches, sometimes adding many inches of silt in a single year. If you have this problem, you should plant a one- or two-row shrub windbreak. Plant it about 100 feet from the ditch and on either or both sides of it. Shrubs suitable for windbreaks include bush honeysuckle, Persian lilac, autumn olive, multiflora rose, and Amur and California privets in the East; caragana, chokecherry, Russian-olive, and squawbush pyrocantha in the West. On peat and muck soils spirea has been successful.

You can keep ditchbanks and berms in grasses and legumes by mowing once a year if the slopes are flat enough, by restricted grazing, or by the use of herbicides.

Do your mowing only after ground-nesting birds have left the nest, usually about grain-harvest time. Avoid overgrazing— it is important to maintain a good grass cover to prevent erosion and siltation of the ditch. Avoid burning—it seldom helps the grasses and often encourages weeds.

Keep woody plants **out;** keep good grasses **in;** plant windbreaks where needed; be careful to do mowing or grazing only in late summer; avoid burning—this is good management both for ditchbanks and game birds.

Odd Land Areas For Game Birds

Parcels of "waste" land that can be changed into land for game birds are called odd areas. They include eroded areas in crop fields, bare knobs, sinkholes, sand blowouts, large gullies, abandoned roads and railroad rights-of-way, borrow pits, gravel pits, and pieces of good land that are cut off from the rest of a field by a stream, drainage ditch, or gully.

Some odd areas already have the kinds of plants that produce good food and cover—they need little or no improvement except protection from fire and grazing. Others may provide nesting cover but no winter cover.

If the odd area you want to improve has no food or cover plants, you will need to add them. In the North, you might well start by planting a winter cover of adapted conifers in the center of the area. Plant 25 to 50 in a solid clump. Space them about 8 feet apart so they will retain their lower limbs and keep good cover close to the ground as long as possible. In Southern areas, where snow is infrequent and temperatures seldom stay below freezing very long, the conifers for winter cover are not needed.

Next, you can supply nesting cover and food by surrounding the conifers with one to three rows of fruit-producing shrubs. These might include multiflora rose, autumn olive, and blackberry, all of which are thorny and make good escape cover too. Multiflora rose would provide emergency food for pheasants. Be sure to leave **at least** half of your odd area in good ground cover of grasses and legumes. Good ground cover is needed by pheasants and other ground-nesting birds. If you want to increase bobwhites in their country you may want to include ⅛ acre or more of shrub lespedeza.

Plant your shrubs 3 to 4 feet apart to get a good thicket. Plant shrub lespedezas in rows 3 feet apart with the plants 2 feet apart in the row.

Working out from the shrubs, you will want to have at least one-half of the area in nesting cover for bobwhites and other ground-nesting birds. If native grasses are sparse, you can sow a mixture of grasses and legumes. Korean, Kobe, and common lespedezas are topnotch bobwhite foods. Don't try to get too heavy a stand—nesting birds like to be able to see what is coming their way. If your soil is acid you will need to apply lime before seeding legumes. Ask your local soil conservationist for help in choosing species to seed and in determining your soil's need for lime and fertilizer.

To keep livestock out of your odd area, you could add a living fence of multiflora rose or other thorny shrub. If you live where living fences do not grow well, you will need a wire fence—the kind will depend on the type of stock.

FARM POND

A pond properly managed can be helpful to game bird propagation.

If you live in the pheasant-producing **area west of the Mis**-sissippi and want to increase pheasants, you may want to make your odd-area planting in the form of a windbreak. Plant two rows of such hardy shrubs as wild plum, sand cherry, Russian-olive, or bush honeysuckle on the west and north sides. Then sow a strip 100 feet wide to sweetclover and plant a block of at least 100 conifers or hardwood trees like green ash, soft maple, or boxelder in the southwest corner. This type of planting should be at least one acre in size to provide the winter shelter and the nesting cover needed in that area.

If you live east of the Great Plains, you can often depend on nature to provide native shrubs in odd areas that are protected from fire and grazing. That means you may need to plant only multiflora rose or a grass-legume mixture.

Plan to spray or mow half of the grassy area every other year to keep woody plants out of it.

Ponds For Game Birds

Ponds provide drinking water for game birds and can also be an area for resting, feeding, and breeding ducks and geese.

Ponds above the local water table must be constructed on tight subsoils or be sealed with clay; otherwise, they will not hold water. They are often built in gullies or small valleys with steep sides and gradually sloping floors so they will hold the desired amount of water without excessive height in the fill. Other ponds are built by excavating and diking the site.

The water supply for most ponds comes from water running off the land. The size of the watershed needed varies according to local rainfall, topography, type of cover, and rate of evaporation. The entire watershed should be in ungrazed woods or improved permanent pasture or range. Cropland in the watershed shortens the life of the pond by allowing too much silt to get into it.

What was said about wetlands for raising game birds also applies here. Depth of the water, available food, and other such items are important.

Ask your local soil conservationist for advice on building your pond. You will profit from his local experience and knowledge.

If possible, the pond should be fenced to keep out livestock. This is important to protect the fill, spillway, and pond banks from trampling; and to provide a filter strip of grass to remove silt from the water before it reaches the pond. Fencing will also

LIVING FENCE

allow you to make plantings for upland game birds, if needed.

In many areas, multiflora rose or other thorny shrubs may be used to establish a fence or hedge as shown in the illustration following.

Also you may want to plant a few clumps of conifers or shrubs. All raw areas above the waterline should be seeded to adapted grasses and shallow-rooted legumes like alsike clover, red clover, or Korean or common lespedeza. Never plant trees, shrubs, or deep-rooted legumes like alfalfa, sweetclover, or sericea lespedeza on the fill.

You might also want to manage your pond for fish production. If so, don't plant anything in the water. Keep woody plants back at least 25 feet from the water's edge to allow plenty of room for fishing.

If you don't care about fish but want to attract waterfowl to your pond, you can add a loafing place in shallow water and allow a few cattails, arrowhead, bulrushes, or burreeds to come in naturally.

Fence Rows And Hedges For Game Birds

Old type rail and stone fences were helpful to game birds because they provided cover of one kind or another close to the farmer's fields where food could be found. The invention of the barbed and woven-wire fences brought easier construction and was less wasteful of cropland, **but,** unless the landowner allowed native shrubs to grow, furnished no cover for game birds.

Now, a new kind of fence is gaining popularity. It is the living fence of close-growing shrubs. Where it is used it is a real boon to game birds. Shrubby fence rows have been shown to harbor fewer harmful and many more beneficial kinds of wildlife than do grassy fence rows, on most farms and ranches.

Multiflora rose is an outstanding shrub for use in fence rows and hedges wherever it can be grown. It is capable of forming a living fence that requires no wire, needs no hard-to-maintain braces to follow contour lines, and does not require trimming or pruning. It is fast growing and attractive, makes good game bird cover, and produces food. Because it sometimes spreads into pastures and abandoned farmland, multiflora rose is unacceptable to some landowners.

Where multiflora rose cannot be grown or is not wanted, one of the following shrubs will produce good hedge or fence-row cover: Red cedar, gray dogwood, American hazelnut, elder, silky cornel, highbush cranberry, bush honeysuckle, Russian-olive, pyrocantha, chokecherry, trifoliate orange, buffaloberry, squawbush, or autumn olive.

Autumn olive is an outstanding producer of food for birds. As a hedge, it makes a screen that shuts out an unpleasant view and discourages trespassers.

If you don't want to grow shrubs in your fence rows, you can improve them for game birds with sericea lespedeza or sweet-clover.

Existing fence rows of shrubs, trees, and vines can be made neat in appearance by cutting out the trees. This also reduces competition with crops.

Border For Game Birds

Game bird borders are used to control erosion and to make use of narrow strips of land in which satisfactory grain crops are hard to grow. They are also used in places where perennial plants are needed for special purposes.

In different parts of the United States such borders are established in one or more of the following situations: As turn-rows along the edges of cropland fields; in sapped areas such as those where cropland is next to woodland or windbreaks; along streams or ditches; around waterways, wet spots, or gullies; along farm roads; above diversion dikes; and for confinement strips to keep Bermuda grass from spreading into cropland fields.

There are really two types of borders: Those made up of grasses and legumes and those of shrubs or shrubs and conifers. Both types benefit game birds by providing either food or cover —sometimes both. The cover they furnish is usually next to cropland where food is sometimes available.

Windbreaks Help Propagate Game Birds

Field windbreaks are planted in crop fields to help control wind erosion and lessen the drying effect of wind on the soil. They conserve snow moisture needed in low rainfall and light soil areas.

Because of the large amount of "edge" in relation to acreage, field windbreaks are especially valuable in providing game bird

WINDBREAK

cover. They create homes for insect-eating birds close to crop-land, where they can do the most good. They also provide cover and travel lanes for game.

Farmstead windbreaks are planted around farm buildings to protect them from winter wind and snow. They are very impor-tant to pheasants in winter.

Two kinds of field windbreaks are used in various parts of the United States. In the prairie areas shrub-hardwood wind-breaks are common; in formerly forested ares pine windbreaks are used.

Both kinds are usually planted at right angles to the prevail-ing wind.

Streambanks For Game Birds

Streambanks are treated to control bank cutting, protect val-uable adjoining property, and reduce the silt load in streams. Such streambank protection is one of the best ways to improve game bird conditions because it usually provides food, cover, and water close together.

On all types of streambank improvement, much of the value for game birds comes from planting moisture-tolerant shrubs and trees between the bank and the fences of adjacent fields. Shrubs that you can use in such places include red-osier dogwood, silky cornel, Russian-olive, nannyberry, and highbush cranberry. Mul-tiflora rose living fenses may be planted as a permanent fence along the top of the streambank.

White pine, yellow pine, Northern white cedar, Rocky Moun-tain juniper, and Norway spruce are conifers you can plant for winter cover.

With the proper management of the areas just described, land owners can have abundant game birds and improve their land at the same time. Every piece of land is a complex com-munity which is successful only if the living things in it are working together. What the raiser of game birds does on his land to maintain the most desirable biologic balance can make the difference between success and failure with game birds.

Chapter II

RAISING GAME BIRDS
IN CAPTIVITY

Whether your objective is a small scale operation to supply hunting and food needs or a full-time business, raising game birds in captivity can be an enjoyable and profitable enterprise. A relatively new practice, it has developed rapidly in recent years and offers a real challenge to people who like to work outdoors, close to nature.

The game bird industry breaks down into three distinct fields: (1) Showing and exhibiting ornamental game birds, as a hobby, (2) operating a public or private shooting preserve as a business, and (3) raising birds for meat production. Where meat production is the objective, game birds are often processed and sold as gift packages or to a specialized institutional trade. As the American standard of living rises, people demand more delicacies and housewives can afford to buy game birds when birds are available. This has opened a new outlet and we now see game bird producers raising exclusively for this purpose.

Much of what was stated in the previous chapter on propagating game birds in open areas applies to birds in captivity. After all, when we raise birds in captivity we are only trying to duplicate or improve upon wild birds in open areas.

One game manager from the State of Wisconsin Department of Natural Resources lists five basic guidelines for raising game birds in open areas worthy of review here. Read and consider them for they will guide and limit how far you can go in raising birds in captivity and feeding them after release. He states:

1. It should be understood that all game species are basically hardy and able to take care of themselves.
2. Winter feeding is recommended primarily to get animals and birds over "rough spots" during extreme weather conditions.
3. Pheasants, quail and Hungarian partridge tend to become too dependent on artificial feeding as a sole source of food when fed for any length of time (two weeks or more).
4. Game birds congregating at feeders become very susceptible to predation and disease.
5. Feeders should be located next to cover to provide escape routes for birds as well as protection from wind.

Keep these guidelines in mind if you are planning to raise game birds; especially if you are inexperienced.

Any person interested in raising game birds should study the industry and its requirements carefully. A beginner should start on a small scale. Visit other operations if that is possible. Established breeders or preserve operators usually welcome visitors. This is a good way to begin learning. For the sake of courtesy, however, always make an appointment before you visit.

A beginner should also write to his State Conservation Agency for laws that govern game bird production. Laws differ from state to state so no attempt has been made to reproduce them here. National game bird associations and publications, as well as the information in this book, will also provide helpful information.

Success in raising game birds is based on four points: (1) Good breeding, (2) Sound management, (3) Careful sanitation, and (4) Good feeding.

Selecting Good Breeding Stock

Regardless of the kind of game birds you plan to raise, start with good, strong breeding stock. When buying eggs or chicks, order from a reputable dealer who has carefully selected or bred healthy birds that produce well. Sometimes it is possible to see parent breeding stock and dressed birds from the strain.

An examination of production and growth records also tell much about the stock you are buying.

Egg production and hatchability are two important factors to keep in mind when selecting breeders. They are important in setting objectives you might try to obtain during the breeding season. Based on reliable research, the following table lists some reasonable goals to work toward.

Table I.   Average Seasonal Egg Production and Hatchability of Fertile Eggs By Type of Hen

Type of Hen	Average Seasonal Egg Production Per Hen	Hatchability Of Fertile Eggs
Chukars	30-50 eggs	90%
Mallards	80-90 eggs	80%
Pheasants	60-70 eggs	85%
Quail	55-65 eggs	90%

When saving breeders from birds you raise, select from strains which most closely meet or surpass the above standards. Selection of breeders should start when chicks are only one day old so you can observe their growth, feathering, and stamina. Any chicks which show promise can be leg-banded as potential breeders. Some breeders actually start the selection of their breeding stock prior to incubation since only chicks from high egg producing hens should be kept for that purpose. They do this by setting eggs from such hens together in separate trays of the incubators. These chicks are raised separately and when fourteen weeks old a selection is made and the best out of this group are kept for future breeders.

Use Sound Management Practices

Numerous management practices contribute to success with game birds. Those recommended here are the more important and should be carefully heeded.

Mating Season— The breeding season naturally comes with spring. Game bird hens will usually produce eggs from early spring to early fall. Hens should be mated with cocks about one month before production is expected to start. For the best fertility, mate one pheasant cock with five to eight hens. Quail and chukars are usually mated in pairs but some producers have successfully mated quail in colonies of one cock to two, three, or four hens. Eggs should be collected several times a day to prevent the birds from breaking and eating them and to avoid chilling or overheating. The ideal egg-holding temperature is 55-56° F. Humidity should range from 70-75%. For best hatchability, eggs should be incubated as soon as possible. It is recommended that they be incubated within one week after they are laid. Eggs held for two weeks or longer do not hatch as well as those placed in an incubator within seven days or less. Much of the difficulty experienced in poor hatchability has been due to the length of time eggs were held as well as improper temperature and humidity during the holding period.

Incubating The Eggs: Temperature, humidity, and ventilation are very important factors in operating an incubator successfully. Be sure plenty of fresh air is allowed to circulate around the incubator in order that embryos will not suffocate from lack of oxygen. Follow the recommendations of the incubator manufacturer for best results. Under normal incubating conditions quail eggs will hatch in about twenty-four days, chukar in approximately twenty-five days, and pheasants from twenty-three to twenty-six days.

Brooding Temperature For Chicks: The hover temperature

should be maintained at 95° F. during the first week. Lower it gradually, 5° a week, for the next three weeks. During warm weather heat is usually not necessary after the first month. However, be careful to avoid chilling which can cause suffocation by crowding.

Floor Space For The Chicks: Overcrowding encourages cannibalism. Give chicks plenty of room. See recommended floor space below.

Table II.   Number of Chicks Per Square Foot of Floor Space

Game Bird	1-10 days	10 days—6 weeks	6-14 weeks
Quail	9	9	3
Chukars	6	3	1
Pheasants and Mallards	4	1	¼

Birds in flight pens need twenty five square feet each. Mallards only need three square feet each in holding pens.

Feeder Space: There are a number of different types of feeders available. Among them, hanging tube-type feeders have become popular and can be used indoors or outside. Recommended feeder space is below:

Table III.   Linear Feeder Space Requirements

Game Bird	1-10 days	10 days—6 weeks	6 weeks and over
Pheasants and Mallards	1 inch	2 inches	3 inches
Quail	½ inch	1 inch	1½ inches
Chukars	¾ inch	1½ inches	2 inches

Water Space: Game birds need a lot of water to grow fast and to stay healthy. Always keep clean, fresh water before them at all times. Birds need more drinking space as they grow. The water space requirements for day-old chicks follows:

Table IV.   Water Space Requirements For Day-Old Chicks

Game Bird	Three 1-gal. water founts will take care of:	Drinking space needed with trough-type waterers
Quail	300 birds	1 ft. per 100 birds
Chukars	200 birds	1 ft. per 50 birds
Pheasants and Mallards	100 birds	1 ft. per 25 birds

Brooder House Litter: The brooder house floor must be kept clean and dry to keep healthy chicks growing fast. Materials that can be used successfully for litter are shavings, ground corn cobs, peanut hulls, and crushed and chopped cornstalks. All must be quite fine and relatively free from dust.

Prevention of Cannibalism: Cannibalism or injurious pecking at each other usually depends on space, cover, and temperament of the birds. When it becomes a problem, debeaking is usually necessary. Chicks may be debeaked when they are one day old with finger nail clippers or with an electric debeaker. If they are debeaked early, chicks may need it again at six weeks and again at twelve to fourteen weeks. For meat birds the upper beaks should be cut back about half way from the tip to the nostril opening at a slight angle. Only the tip of the lower beak should be removed. For birds that will be released into open areas, use the block debeaking method—

cut both upper and lower beak square across about one-fourth from the tip.

Shelter For Older Birds: When birds are grown for release it is best to move them from the brooder house to flight pens at the end of their sixth week. Small shelters will protect the birds from driving rain and hot sun and tends to "harden" them for the open fields in which they must survive. Planted cover, such as, grain sorghum, sunflowers, and weeds in the pens will also provide shade and necessary cover.

Production Cost Records: Items on which you will need to keep records to figure total production costs include chick cost, labor, feed cost, medication, depreciation on facilities and equipment, insurance on the facilities and birds, utilities, litter cost, repairs and maintenance cost, and interest on operating capital and taxes. The cost of production is the only intelligent way to sell birds for release or for the market and is the only way in which you can tell whether or not the enterprise is making money for you.

Sanitation Is Important

Several simple rules of sanitation should be carried out to keep your game birds free from disease, parasites, and infection.

Before starting chicks, houses and all equipment should be thoroughly cleaned and disinfected. A disinfectant cleaner should be used to wash all equipment after which it is recommended that all clean surfaces be disinfected to kill disease producing bacteria, viruses, and fungi. A concentrate recommended for the purpose should be used to treat the floor to kill coccidia, worm eggs, and other micro-organisms. This should be done on a dirt floor as well as one made of wood. Cleanliness takes time but can be your best preventative against disease. Disinfectant and cleaning supplies can generally be purchased from any supplier selling game bird or poultry feed and equipment.

The spread of disease through drinking water in quart, gallon or automatic founts can be prevented by treating the water with one of several materials on the market for this purpose. Flies should be kept under control as much as possible and rats and mice should be kept away from the premises. Rats and mice are disease carriers and will even kill chicks when they are young.

Roundworms can also be a problem. Treat breeders for worms a few weeks before production begins to avoid stress during the laying season. Controlling worms can save feed costs. As much as possible, try to keep chicks on clean ground.

In case you have an outbreak of coccidiosis, paratyphoid, typhoid or fowl cholera, treat the flock immediately. Most poultry supply stores carry a recommended treatment or you may contact your veterinarian. In the event of blackhead, ulcerative, or enteritis, see your local veterinarian or ship typically affected specimens of your birds to the nearest state poultry diagnostic laboratory. Follow the advice they give you.

Use A Good Feeding Program

To grow well-feathered, active, and healthy game birds, chicks must be well fed and good feeding must continue until maturity. Several companies now manufacture feed especially formulated for game birds. A ration for game birds only is recommended over one for poultry if it can be obtained. Game bird feeds are scientifically designed for specific types of birds based on long and careful research. This fact is tremendously important. For example, it takes a quail chick four days to eat a thimbleful of feed. When you consider this, you can quickly see why every bag of feed must be milled with a maximum degree of critical precision. Feed manufacturers are doing this with a great deal of accuracy and at a cost much lower than could be done with a "home-mix."

More details on feeding are given in the chapters for specific types of game birds.

Chapter III

PHEASANT PROPAGATION

The sixteen distinct groups, or genera, of pheasants include the Junglefowls, ancestors of domestic poultry, the Argus, and Peafowls. All but one are native to Asia. There are 173 different kinds (species and sub-species) in the sixteen genera. With few exceptions, all pheasants live and breed well in captivity.

Pheasant-raising is, by odds, the most popular type of game farming. The pheasant is chosen because of its multi-color and because it is relatively easy to raise.

Since it is common, most widely used for shooting preserves, and an excellent bird for meat production, the Chinese Ring-Neck Pheasant will be emphasized in this book. Other pheasants raised for ornamental, hobby, or other purpose include:

Amherst Pheasant	Mongolian Pheasant
Blue Earned Pheasant	Palawan Peacock-Pheasant
Cheer Pheasant	Reeve's Pheasant
Edward's Pheasant	Siamese Fireback Pheasant
Golden Pheasant	Silver Pheasant
Green Junglefowl	Star Tragopan
Impeyan Pheasant	Swinhoe's Pheasant
Malayan Fireback Pheasant	Versicolor Pheasant
Mikado Pheasant	White Crested Kaliji Pheasant

Some of these kinds of pheasants are uncommon, and a few are even rare. If you prefer to raise one of these uncommon species, what is written here about Chinese Ring-Necks will generally also apply to them.

What was given about raising game birds in captivity and in the open in previous chapters also apply to pheasants, but the following will deal specifically with pheasants.

It can be said at the start that almost anyone who has the will to secure proper equipment and follow a few basic rules of management can successfully brood and rear ring-necked pheasants. There are no "cut and dried" formulas which will assure success to everyone who makes an attempt. However, the following information and suggestions are fundamental.

Should You Start With Eggs?

Because of the work involved and experience necessary in working with brood hens or incubators, it is recommended that a beginner start with chicks. He will generally find that the amount of labor and cost will be substantially less and that he will achieve much better results. However, it must be said that some breeders have done a very good job of hatching pheasant eggs themselves.

The first eggs may be expected from pheasant hens about April first to fifteenth. It is wise when ordering hatching eggs to place your order with the breeder well in advance of this date so that you can have an early hatch.

Upon arrival from the breeder, or from your own hens, eggs may be held for a few days if necessary, but it is advisable to set or incubate them sooner. Upon receipt of pheasant eggs, unpack all of them and place them point or small end down in a shallow tray or pan containing sand or grain. They should be allowed to settle for at least twenty-four hours before giving them to the hen or placing in an incubator for hatching. It is very important that they be stored in a cool place where a temperature of from fifty to sixty degrees is maintained. A cellar usually makes a good place for storage. During storage, the eggs should be turned daily to keep the germ alive; however, the point or small end should always be kept down and the egg merely tilted in one direction one day and the opposite the next.

Always try to get your eggs for hatching before they are ten days old; the fresher they are, the better results you will obtain. Also, if possible, always try to keep together all the eggs of the same size and species so they will hatch at the same time.

Before receiving your eggs all preparations should be made either for an incubator or for the use of bantam or medium weight setting hens. Bantams are commonly used for hatching eggs if no incubator is available. The Silkies and Cochins are highly recommended but Sebrights make good mothers and are often favored for their lighter weight over the heavier bantams. Rhode Island Reds, Wyandottes, and Plymouth Rock hens generally make good foster mothers, but Leghorns, Anconas, and Minorcas should never be used.

While it is important that you have a source for obtaining setting hens before the eggs are expected, do not get hens until you are notified when the eggs are to be shipped. Setting hens will "break up" if they are held too long before a setting of eggs is given to them. A complete discussion of using brood hens will be included later in this chapter.

Artifical incubation has proven successful but you must carefully follow instructions recommended for operating the incubator. The proper balance of heat, humidity, and ventilation must be carefully maintained. Carefully read and follow the instruction book that came with the incubator. If buying a new incubator, small units especially designed for game birds are now available. Such a type is highly recommended.

Breeding of Pheasants

There are two basic systems of breeding pheasants to produce hatching eggs—the small pen system and the large pen system.

Small Pen System

Breeding Ratio. The small pen or "harem" system of breeding pheasants is used on many game farms in the United States. Five or six hens and one cock bird are placed in a movable pen twelve feet square and six feet high. Top of the pen may be covered with a two-inch mesh, nineteen gauge wire netting. The pen should be boarded at least twenty inches from the bottom to provide necessary protection.

Feeding and Watering. To avoid unnecessary disturbance to the pheasants while feeding, it is desirable to feed and water from outside the pen. A hopper having two sections—one for mash and grain and another for grit, charcoal, and oyster shells —is placed on the outside and a horizontal slot cut in the board base to enable the birds to reach through for the food. Pheasants require a laying mash having a high protein content. Most commercial turkey laying mashes may be fed with good results. Some feed companies also manufacture special feeds for pheasants. For water, a water pan is placed next to the feeding hopper. A vertical slot in the board base is used in connection with the water pan, as a horizontal one prevents the birds from tipping back their heads when drinking. It is very important that a fresh supply of water be kept before the birds at all times.

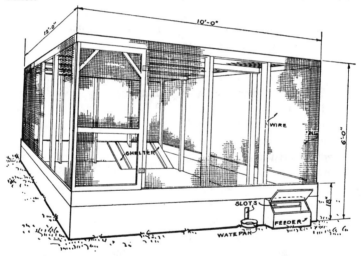

Pheasant Breeding Pen showing outside feeder and waterer.

Shelter. To provide shade and protection from storms and other poor weather conditions, a small shelter two feet wide by three feet long should be built in one corner of the pen. In many cases, pheasant hens will lay their eggs under these shelters, so it is advisable to hinge them to one side of the pen so that they may be lifted to enable removing the eggs from underneath with little difficulty. If breeding pens are used to hold birds during the winter, additional brush or cornshock shelters should be provided.

Breeding pheasants should be placed in breeding pens about March 1 in Wisconsin and other northern states. The pens should be moved to fresh ground at least three times during the breeding season. This will aid in maintaining a fresh supply of green food, as green food should be available at all times during mating season.

Large Pen System

Breeding Ratio. The large or open pen system is also used widely in game farming. Under this plan, it is customary to place one hundred hens and fifteen to twenty cocks in a pen, allowing at least one hundred square feet per bird. Such pens are enclosed by a seven or eight foot fence having a two foot strand of three-fourths inch wire on the lower part and two inch mesh wire on the upper portion of the fence. The small mesh wire should be buried at least six to twelve inches in the ground to keep out undesirable pests.

The equipment cost in the large pen system is perhaps less, but results are not usually as satisfactory as the small pen systems. In the large pen system, egg production is, as a rule, lower and much trouble is experienced in controlling predacious animals and birds due to the fact that the pens do not have a wire covering on the top.

Feeding and Watering. Feeding and watering in the large pen system is a much different procedure. Ordinary commercial feeding hoppers and waterers may be placed throughout the pen. The food mixtures, however, are the same. If ordinary watering pans are used, a covering should be built over them in order to prevent contamination. Again, a plentiful supply of fresh water must be kept in front of the birds at all times.

Shelter. Lean-to or cornshock shelters should be erected in the large breeding pen to provide shade and protection from sto m.

Egg Production. While pheasant hens lay a few eggs during the month of April, heavy production cannot be expected until the middle of May. Pheasant hens will usually average from thirty to forty eggs during the laying period. Early and mid-season eggs have the highest fertility and produce the strongest chicks. Eggs late in the season may not be fertile at all.

Egg Collection. Great care must be taken not to disturb pheasants any more than is absolutely necessary when gathering eggs. To avoid startling the birds, many game breeders whistle while working around the pens. Be careful to avoid sudden movements while working in or around the pen.

Eggs should be collected once a day during the early part of the season and twice daily during hot weather. After eggs are collected, they should be stored in a cool room and handled as was explained earlier in this chapter.

Artificial Brooding

Types of Equipment: Many types of brooding equipment have proven to be satisfactory. Some of the common types recommended are discussed in the following materials.

Brooder House: One type of brooder house is a small double brooder house with a screen porch. Dimensions are six feet long, seven feet wide, and three feet high. The house is insulated throughout and has a combined capacity of 300 pheasant chicks, depending on the type of brooder to be used. Brooders for this type of house can be two small box types or small canopy type electric units with at least a 500 watt heating unit. The amount of heat required may of course be less in southern states than in the north. The capacity of each box type unit is 150 chicks. The approximate size of the canopy type is 20 x 30 inches which will handle 175 chicks.

Temperature of Brooder. The brooder temperature should be regulated to maintain an even one hundred degrees (100°) on the floor. The current should be turned on twenty-four hours before the chicks are to arrive, and the temperature rechecked to be absolutely sure that the thermostats are properly regulated. The temperature of 100 degrees should be the temperature of the hover near the outside edge **on the floor.** It is suggested that the thermometer be placed on the floor, as many commercial hovers have the thermometer extending from three to as high as six inches in the air.

Shelter Pens. In conjunction with both types of houses, shelter pens are required. In the event that the small double house is used, two shelter pens, twelve by twelve by six, are required and for the large brooder house a shelter pen, twelve by twenty-four by six, is necessary. The shelter pens are boarded at least twenty to twenty-four inches from the ground to protect young birds from driving rains and drafts. The sides of the pen must be wired with a one inch mesh, nineteen gauge netting. It is advisable to cover the top of the pen with a water proof covering as the shelter pen must shed water. The shelter pen is very important, as it is used as a shelter when birds no longer use the house and serves as adequate protection in case of storms.

Runs. The most essential part of the brooder system is the large run. Because of the cost involved in building proper sized runs, many persons try to skimp on the size to find the value involved in losses resulting from cannibalism and from overcrowding far exceed the original cost of the equipment necessary.

Should the small double house be used, two runs are required. Each should measure approximately 25 feet wide by 150 feet long. These runs should be covered on the top. It is advisable to have the side fence of one inch mesh wire and the top covering of two inch mesh wire. In building the runs, it is more practical to have them long and narrow rather than square as it is a much simpler task to cover them with wire, and it is a much easier problem to drive birds in the event it is necessary to hurry them in if a storm should occur.

Should the large house described below be used, the large run is not partitioned. It should measure approximately 50 feet wide by 150 feet long. The wire netting of the side fence should be of one inch mesh while the top covering can be of two inch mesh.

Many types of brooder houses and pens are satisfactory. However, the types of equipment suggested above have been thoroughly proven. The pen dimensions given provides the required 20 square feet per chick and standard 150 foot rolls of 6 foot netting can be used satisfactorily without waste when runs are covered.

Large Type Brooder House. Also practical is the large house or ordinary poultry brooder house. The dimensions should be about twelve feet long, ten feet wide and six feet high. This house should also be insulated and properly ventilated. The brooder capacity of a house of this size is 350 pheasants.

Brooder for Large House Type. Any type of commercial

hover or canopy style brooder may be used in the large house; either oil, gas or electric. However, the use of coal brooders is not recommended. An electric or gas brooder is usually depended upon to furnish a more uniform heat. Capacity of the hover must be at least five hundred chick size.

Preparation Of Equipment

Preparation of the House. The brooder house should be thoroughly disinfected to help prevent disease and parasites. Only commercial disinfectant is satisfactory. An inexpensive solution consists of a small can of lye mixed with sixteen gallons of water. Do not mix this solution in a metal pail and you must be very careful to keep it off of your skin. Severe burns can occur if this isn't done. The house should be thoroughly scrubbed and allowed to dry. The entire floor should then be covered with litter about two inches thick.

Litter. Any good litter can be used satisfactorily. Pine shavings (but not sawdust), peat moss, or cotton seed hulls are some of the materials that can be used. Regardless of the type used, it is necessary to spread litter over the entire brooder house floor about two inches thick. This keeps the chicks from scratching down to the floor where they find and eat small indigestible particles which may cause the gizzard to become impacted and result in starvation. If the small double type brooder house is used, the litter must be covered with light colored cloth, white preferable, placed in front and extending one-third of the way under the brooder. The cloth may be white or light colored feed bags. If a canopy type brooder is used, the entire space inside of the circle which is used to confine the chicks to the brooder must be covered with light colored cloth or rough surface paper. Regardless of the type of brooder used the cloth should be continued for five or six days and changed daily.

Sprinkle a generous amount of chick feed on the cloth and place at least five small chick feeders and five two-quart jar type fountains inside of circle for large type brooders and two of each in small type. Some people use shallow paper plates as feeders the first few days. After five or six days discontinue both the cloth and the circle. At this time the feeders and fountains should be placed on two raised frames made of 1" x 4" lumber and covered with one-half inch hardware cloth. These can later be used in the shelter pens.

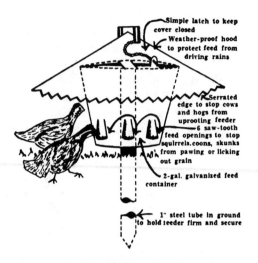

A popular field quail feeder.

Guard. In order that pheasant chicks can be confined close to the hover, a guard of metal, wire screen or even corrugated paperboard should be used in the small type of house and placed approximately twelve inches from the brooder. The canvas flap on the brooder should be up about two inches from the cloth on the floor to allow the chicks a free run to and from it. The guard is discontinued after the first day and chicks are allowed the entire brooder house floor space. In the case of the canopy type brooder, a guard about sixteen inches in height should be placed approximately a foot from the brooder proper so chicks cannot wander too far away from the source of heat. This guard should be constructed so that it can be made longer as the chicks grow older and expanded accordingly.

Feeding

Type of Feed. The successful rearing of pheasants depends to a great extent upon the use of the proper ration, especially during the first two or three weeks. Recent experiments indicate that starting and growing mashes having a high protein content are satisfactory. Most commercial turkey starting and growing mashes are adequate. However, in the case of a starting feed, a starting mash in a small kernel form is the most desirable and is a type of food that pheasant chicks will be inclined to start eating immediately.

Feeding. Starting mash can be fed to pheasants up to the time they are from three to four weeks of age. From that time on, they may be fed on a growing mash. Starting and growing mashes usually contain the same ingredients, but the growing mash is in a larger kernel form to prevent waste. A good rule of thumb followed by some raisers is to put out enough feed so that the birds will clean it up in about 30 to 45 minutes. Any more feed than this will be more than they need and is a loss.

After young pheasants are approximately six weeks of age, a small amount of grain may be added to the feed. This is increased gradually until the ration consists of approximately one-fourth grain and three-fourths mash up to the end of the tenth week. Green food should be supplied at all times. Cabbage, rape and chopped lettuce can and should be supplied to young pheasants during the first week and thereafter until they can actually secure a plentiful supply of green food which should be present in the shelter pen and large run.

Watering. Fresh water should be kept in front of the birds at all times. Water given to chicks for the first time should have the chill removed, as cold water will kill day-old chicks. Stones and pebbles should be placed in the trough during the first few days to keep chicks from waddling in the water.

Cover Crop

Preparation of Shelter Pen and Run. A cover crop should be planted in the shelter pen and large run. Rape, alfalfa and clover make excellent cover crops. Rape is perhaps the most practical as it has a sturdier stem, is fast growing and provides an abundance of green food, and it is difficult for the birds to kill it out. Rape can be broadcast at the rate of about twelve pounds to the acre.

If, by the time the chicks arrive, the cover crop is too heavy, strips should be mowed throughout the pen to give the ground a chance to sweeten and enable the birds to move about more readily.

In the event there is no cover crop in the shelter pen or run, fresh green food in the form of chopped lettuce, cabbage or alfalfa hay should be provided. Green food should never be piled as this will cause fermentation, and would be detrimental to the chicks.

Shelter. It is necessary that small lean-to shelters be erected in the large run to provide sufficient shade and protection from storms, if there is not adequate natural ground cover.

Management Practices In Rearing Pheasants

You should have your brooder operating and maintaining a uniform temperature of one hundred degrees Fahrenheit (100°F.) on the floor at least twenty-four hours before the chicks arrive. Litter, as has been explained, should cover the entire floor of the brooder house, and white cloth should be placed in front of the brooder or around and under the hover depending upon the type of brooder unit to be used.

Starting feed should be sprinkled liberally on the cloth, on several shallow paper plates or egg flats. A supply of lukewarm water should be available together with a number of two quart or gallon watering jars with pebbles in the troughs.

Arrival of Chicks. When the chicks arrive, they should be placed underneath the brooder or hover. In most cases, many will start eating immediately. They will seem very active if the temperature is correct. Watering jars can then be placed around the hover, but keep them several inches away from the chick guard.

First Twenty-Four Hours. If the small double house is used, the chicks should have about 12 inches of space directly in front of the brooder. After the first day the guard may be placed on top of the brooder to keep chicks from getting up on the brooder. They can be given the run of the space afforded by the removal of the chick guard. One important rule to remember is to always check the floor temperature carefully.

In the case of the canopy type brooder, the guard that encircles the hover will confine the chicks close enough to the heat. The screen necessary for the small type unit should be used the first twenty-four hours and then the chicks will find the heat and will brood properly. However, with the canopy type brooder, you will find that they will brood properly if not confined too closely to the unit. It is advisable to check the last thing each night until chicks discontinue to use the brooder as they may leave the brooder and pile in the corners.

After Fifth Day. The small double house previously described has a screen porch. After the fifth day, providing the weather is favorable, chicks may be permitted to use this porch. When they are in this area, one of the two feeders and waterers that were used inside the house, should be placed on the porch. Chicks, however, should be driven in at night for at least the first three to five days, and the door of the house should be closed. This door, however, should be opened again early in the morning.

In the case of the large brooder house, the chick guard can be removed completely and the chicks permitted to have the run of the entire house. If the chicks at this time are eating from the hoppers, the white cloth or bags can be removed. Be absolutely sure that all chicks are eating, however, before this step is taken.

If the chicks are to be confined in the brooder house after the use of the cloth has been discontinued, the small feeders and waterers should be placed on a raised one-half inch mesh wire screen until they are allowed the use of the shelter pen.

After Twelfth Day. If the weather is very mild, chicks may be permitted to use the shelter pen. They, however, must be driven back into the house at night for several days. It is essential that they be taught to go to and from the shelter pen to the house before all the doors may be left open. Large feeders and waterers should be provided in the shelter pen at this time, and placed up off the ground on a wire screen so the birds do not come in contact with any wet or moldy feed.

Four Weeks of Age. At four weeks of age, pheasants are usually given access to the large run. They, however, should be driven back into the shelter pens several nights. At this stage, the doors to the brooder house or porch should always be left open. In the event of a storm, the birds should be driven into the shelter pen also.

At this time the temperature under the hover should gradually be lowered at the rate of five degrees per week. The temperature, however, should be regulated at all times according to the birds' actions. If they are inclined to start piling up, they are cold; if they pant and their wings are droopy, the temperature is too high. Watching the birds carefully will help you make judgments concerning the correct temperature.

After four weeks, starting mash can gradually be replaced by a growing mash. Feed hoppers should be kept filled. An ample supply of fresh water should be in as many places as possible. The use of many feeders and waterers will discourage congregating, and help eliminate the tendency toward cannibalism. A quantity of grit, charcoal, and oyster shells should also be supplied at this time. When green plants have been entirely consumed within the shelter pen, it is advisable to lime the soil and turn it over with a spade. Brush can then be added in the shelter pens.

Six to Ten Weeks of Age. During the seventh week, a small amount of whole grain may be added to the feed. This can be increased gradually until the ration consists of approximately one-fourth grain and three-fourths mash. It will not be necessary at this stage to drive birds into the shelter pen. Some of them will roost out in the large pens, and therefore, additional shelters should be provided for this purpose. In the event of a damp, rainy season, it is advisable not to permit the cover crop in the large runs to become too thick.

Preparation of the Birds For Liberation. If you plan to release your birds into open areas, this may usually be done from the tenth to the fourteenth week, depending upon the physical condition of the birds. However, it should be remembered that birds should not be released until they are fully feathered. They should have full-tail feathers and full-wing feathers and must be well able to take care of themselves.

When catching birds for release, it is recommended that you drive a portion of them into the shelter pens and use an ordinary landing net to catch them. Great care should be taken at all times so as not to injure the birds. In removing the birds from the net, grasp both legs. This is very important as the legs and wings are easily broken. Birds can then be placed in crates for transportation to the stocking sites.

Range System Of Hatching And Rearing

For many years the accepted method of hatching and rearing pheasants is what is commonly known as the range system. Under this plan, either bantams or medium-weight hens are used as foster mothers. Very satisfactory results may be secured under this system and birds may be raised at low cost if proper management and judgment is exercised. The "broody hen" method is usually on a smaller scale, and capital costs are much less.

Hatching Nest Box Construction. Nest boxes for setting hens should be approximately fourteen inches square and well ventilated but with no holes or openings in the sides through which the baby pheasants might escape after hatching. The box should have an entrance opening, of course, but be fairly dark with a waterproof top. As pheasant eggs require a great deal of moisture, the nest box should have no bottom but should be placed directly on the ground in some shady spot. Concrete or dirt floors of a building are also usually suitable. About four inches of moist soil is put in the box and a slightly concave nest depression hollowed out and lined with a nesting material such as June Grass or hay that isn't too coarse.

Setting Hens. Bantams, Silkies, Cochins, Sebrights, Rhode Island Reds, Wyandottes, and Plymouth Rocks make excellent foster mothers, but Leghorns, Anconas, and Minorcas should never be used. The hen should be tested on china eggs (glass eggs) for about forty-eight hours before she is given a setting of pheasant eggs.

Dusting. The hens must be properly dusted during the incubation period. Many young pheasants may be lost if this isn't done. If you carefully follow the instructions given on recommended dusts, no birds should be lost from lice, fleas, or ticks. The dust that is used should not contain D.D.T. Read the label to be sure.

If the rearing coop isn't new, it should be scraped and brushed clean of all debris. A spray solution that does not contain D.D.T. available from poultry supply dealers, should be sprayed in the coop. Particular attention being paid to the cracks or crevices. If the spray used is in a water solution be certain that the coop is thoroughly dry before it is used. The hen should be dusted with any good poultry dusting powder before she is given the eggs and again on about the fifteenth day. Be certain the entire bird is dusted—paying particular attention to areas around the vent, on the hip, under the wings, on the neck and top of the head. Care must be taken not to get any of the dusting powder in the hen's eyes or nasal openings.

Removing Hen From Nest. The hen should not be permitted to leave the nest at will but is transferred to a feeding crate or coop once a day during the incubation period to be fed and watered. She should be handled slowly and gently at all times. In moving the hen, grasp her gently but firmly with the thumbs over the wings and the fingers around the legs to prevent her from breaking any eggs with her feet.

Feed For The Setting Hen. Whole corn is the best type of feed, although wheat may be added during extremely warm weather. A small amount of grit and charcoal as well as a supply of fresh water should also be given to her. It is very important to make certain that eggs do not become chilled at any time during the incubation. The first two days are the most critical as the embryo is just beginning to develop at this time. The hen may be left off for about fifteen minutes the first week, twenty minutes the second, and from twenty minutes to half an hour the third, depending, of course, upon the weather.

Sprinkling. During the incubation period, which varies from twenty-two to twenty-four days, it is advisable to frequently wet the ground around the nest box. The eggs themselves should be well sprinkled daily with lukewarm water from the twenty-first day until they begin to pip. This should be done just before the hen is put back on the nest. In extremely dry weather, the eggs may be sprinkled two or three times previously to the twenty-first day.

Hatching Time. When the eggs begin to pip, the nest box should be re-examined to make certain that there are no cracks or holes through which the young birds may escape. The hen must not be disturbed while the eggs are hatching. Empty shells should not be removed, nor should chicks be taken from the box until they are thoroughly dry.

Moving from Hatching Box to Brooder Coop. To avoid chiling, it is advisable to move the chicks from the hatching box to the rearing coop between nine o'clock in the morning and two o'clock in the afternoon, the warmest part of the day. It is important that the hen be well fed before being placed in the coop, otherwise she is apt to do a great deal of scratching in search of food with the result that chicks are sometimes injured.

While the hen is eating, the chicks should be kept in a warm place. They may be placed in a bushel basket, the bottom of which is covered with excelsior. The top of the basket can be covered with a cloth. After eating, the hen should be placed in the rearing coop with one or two chicks and given an opportunity to quiet down. The remainder of the chicks may then be placed in the coop with her. Do not disturb the hen for the next ten or twenty minutes. After that, quietly approach the coop to see if the pheasants are being brooded by her. It is also very important to check the coop the last thing in the evening to make certain all chicks are under the hen, and if not, slowly and gently place them underneath the hen by hand.

Rearing Coop. Several types of rearing coops are used. The types recommended especially are those having either a shed or A-type roof. The coops should be approximately thirty-six inches long, twenty inches wide and twenty-four inches high. The top and sides must be waterproof. Vertical bars spaced three and one-half inches apart permit the chicks to range in and out at will but at the same time confine the hen to the coop.

Several days before the hatch is due, the coop should be placed on a level, well-drained spot from which all stubble and stone have been removed. Any tall grass or weeds within six feet of the coop should also be cut to prevent the chicks from getting lost. It is advisable to spread a burlap bag under the coop to prevent the hen from scratching and killing the chicks. To aid in keeping the chicks warm and dry in wet weather, tar paper may be placed under the burlap.

Small Run. A run is provided by attaching two boards thirty to thirty-six inches long and twelve inches high to the front of the coop in the form of a V. It is important that this run and the coop be well banked with dirt to prevent the chicks from getting out. They are confined to the run for about two or three days.

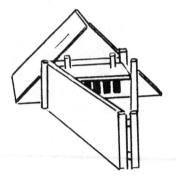

An A-type rearing coop with boards attached to form a V-shaped run.

Instructions On Range System Of Rearing Pheasants

Non-Confinement Plan. The most successful rearing system for the small breeder is the non-confinement plan under which the pheasant chicks are closely confined for the first two or three days, after which the run is removed and they are given free range. The hen is not permitted to run with the chicks. It is important that the coop be shifted to clean ground each day.

Confinement Plan. This system is recommended in instances where the birds are being reared in backyards and other localities where predatory birds and animals cannot be controlled. The hen, as in the non-confinement plan, is kept in the rearing coop at all times, but after the small V-shaped run has been removed the chicks are given the run of a pen approximately twelve feet long, four feet wide and from five to six feet high. A door large enough to admit a person should be constructed in this pen. The base of the pen should be boarded up to a height of from one to one and a half feet and the balance of the pen, including the top, covered with three-quarter or one inch mesh wire. To avoid the danger of diseases resulting from contaminated ground and to furnish the young chicks with an ample supply of green food, the pen should be so constructed that it may be moved at frequent intervals.

Feeding. Whether the chicks are reared under the confinement or non-confinement methods, the feeding schedule is the same. As in the case of birds raised in brooders, starting and growing feed mashes having a high protein content are desirable. Most commercial turkey starting and growing mashes are satisfactory, although the starting feed should be in a small kernel form, if possible. Some major feed companies now manufacture special game feed. This should be used if possible.

This starting mash should be in a small feeder placed close enough to the coop so that the hen may partake of the feed, as well as the chicks. She will teach them how to eat. A water fountain containing fresh water from which the chill has been removed should also be placed adjacent to the brood coop so the foster mother may teach them to drink. It is advisable to disinfect all water used for drinking purposes. A good disinfectant for this purpose can be purchased from a farm supply store selling poultry and/or game supplies. After the chicks learn to eat from the small feed hopper, it should be removed from the reach of the mother. Green food should be provided if a natural supply is not available. About the fourth week, a quantity of grit and fine oyster shells should also be fed. From the fourth week on, the starting mash is gradually replaced by growing mash.

After the fifth week, a commercial scratch grain may be fed in the ration. The amount may be increased gradually until the ration consists of approximately one-fourth grain and three-fourths mash at about the time they are liberated.

Wing Clipping. In the event that birds are not confined in a pen where the top is covered, it will be necessary to clip after they reach the age of two weeks. The birds should be clipped every two weeks thereafter until about three weeks previous to the time they are liberated. At this time, the stub feathers should be pulled to insure full growth of new feathers. However, if birds are only clipped once, it will not be necessary to pull the stub feathers. In the event that the confinement plan is used, a landing net should be used in catching them, and care should be taken so as not to injure them.

Removal of Hen. When young pheasants are from five to seven weeks of age, they will begin to leave the hen at which time she may be removed. Shelter in addition to the coop should then be provided for the young pheasants.

Liberation. Usually young birds are able to shift for themselves between the ages of ten and fourteen weeks. However, the age is not always the determining factor. Young pheasants can be released when good judgment tells you that they are well able to care for themselves.

Instructions For Clipping and Brailing

Wing Clipping

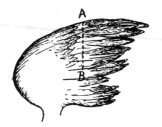

Wing Clipping—cut main flight feathers along line A to B. It is not necessary to clip the wing close.

When catching birds for clipping, an ordinary landing net should be used, and great care taken at all times not to injure the birds. When using a net, permit the birds to run into the net and not manipulate it in a sweeping motion. In removing them from the net, grasp the bird by both legs. This is very important as the legs are easily broken. Hold the bird securely. With the two legs between the third and little finger, place the thumb over the head of the bird and spread the wing with the index finger and the thumb. Then clip the first eight flight feathers with an ordinary scissors. **It is not necessary to clip the wing too close.** See the illustration below.

Brailing

A pheasant brail is a leather strap that measures approximately eight and one-half inches in length and one-half inch in width. One end of the brail is slit. The brail is made of soft leather or plastic so as not to injure the wing of the bird. Brails may be split down about one and one-half inches from one end. They may either be made or purchased at approximately five cents each. It is not advisable to attempt to brail young pheasants because their wings are growing constantly. Such a device and the proper method of attaching it are shown in the following illustration.

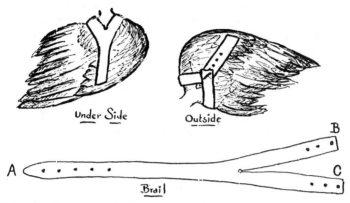

Wing Brailing—a method to prevent flight but not injure wing of pheasants.

Take the split ends of the brail and pass them around the shoulder of the bird so that the ends meet at the top of the shoulder. Take long end, A, and slip it between the first and second flight feathers, bringing it around to meet the split ends, B and C. Adjust brail to allow the wing about half play but not enough for proper flight. Fasten ends, A, B and C, with a brass split pin with prongs facing out.

If birds are penned for a long period, brails must be changed from one wing to another about every three weeks to one month.

Instructions For Pulling Stub Feathers

Use a landing net to catch birds and take great care not to injure them. Grasp them by both legs when removing them from the net. Hold the bird with its head toward you and spread the wings with the thumb and first finger of the same hand. Use a plier or the fingers to pull the stub feathers and pull upward. Care should be taken not to pull a blue or blood feather as this may induce bleeding and cannibalism may develop. Blue or blood feathers grow more rapidly than others.

Stocking

If best results are to be obtained from a propagation program, it is essential that all birds be stocked in cover that best meets their requirements. Suitable cover includes dense thickets of brush, grass or weeds. It is important that all areas stocked have an abundance of cover which will provide shelter during the winter and also some winter feed if possible or the cover should be adjacent to some type of available winter feed. Read the first chapter in this book to get more information on this practice.

Birds should be transported to stocking sites in a well ventilated crate, padded on the top to prevent injury to the birds' heads. In catching the birds for crating, a landing net may be used, care being taken not to injure the birds.

It is advisable to erect a feeding hopper for released birds and supply feed that will give the birds a chance to accustom themselves to the natural food supply. The establishing of a feeding hopper also tends to simplify selection of winter feeding stations, as in most cases birds will frequent this hopper, and a winter feeding program can follow through as soon as cold weather sets in.

In releasing pheasants from a crate, do not open the slot on the crate until the birds have had time to settle down. This helps to prevent injury. Do not attempt to handle the birds but let them wander away of their own accord. The less they are disturbed the more likely they are to remain in the cover adjacent to the point of their release.

Winter Feeding

Feeding stations should be established early in order that the birds will be familiar with their location and will have no difficulty in finding a supply of feed in the advent of heavy snows or sleet storms. There are several excellent types of feeding stations including standing or shocked corn, hoppers protected by lean-to or teepee shelters and pole racks having ears of corn jabbed on spikes driven through the poles from the underside.

It is essential that stations be adjacent to good cover and that they be erected in locations affording maximum protection from drifting snow. The ordinary feeding mixture is two parts whole shelled corn to one part wheat. Some prefer to add to this a percentage of buckwheat. Two per cent of ordinary poultry grit should be added to the ration.

Feeding hoppers may be constructed of any size with either one or two feeding sides. Detailed and illustrated information regarding the various types of feeding stations and plans for feeding hoppers best suited for you may generally be secured by writing to conservation organizations or agencies located in your state.

A wire basket made of two inch mesh poultry netting is a good method of feeding ear corn. It can be fastened to a tree or post to prevent tipping and covering with snow, and should be placed in a good cover area.

Food Patch Planting. Considerable experimental work has been done with food patches. Various grains have been used, but it is believed at the present time that standing corn is the most reliable all-around type of food patch. Buckwheat serves as an excellent type of food patch also, but is of very little help in the time of heavy snow. Some of the sorghums are good, especially during dry seasons. Due to the fact that almost as good soil and as much cultivation is required to insure a good crop of sorghum, we recommend that corn be used. While corn may be left standing, it is necessary that buckwheat be cut and bundled, and, if possible, fed on racks of poles above snow level.

The success of a feeding program depends a great deal upon its being started early enough so that food is available for the birds before they are actually in need of it. Food patches furnish such a supply. We cannot depend entirely upon them, but during the average winter they will simplify winter feeding to a great extent.

Diseases and Parasites

Pheasants are subject to many of the diseases and parasites common to poultry. Since treatment in most cases is almost impossible, the important thing here is to prevent diseases and parasites before they occur. Little difficulty should be experienced in the raising of pheasants up to the time of liberation if the following procedures are followed.

1. Keep Clean, Dry Litter in the Brooder House. Moldy litter contains spores that are inhaled by the young birds. These, in turn, not only produce a gangrenous necrotic (wasting away) pneumonia but also develop in the air sacs eventually resulting in death. Infections of nearly any nature may develop from unsanitary conditions which also promote the development of parasites. Concentration of birds in a given area means parasitism. The means of prevention is the following of strict sanitary measures with special regard to the litter.

2. Maintain an Even Temperature and Do Not Chill or Overheat the Birds. Avoid Drafts. The results of exposure of young pheasants to variations in temperature and drafts can be readily seen on post-mortem examination, as the lungs are no longer the normal rosy-pink color but in many cases becomes bluish and solidified. Many of the birds will die from exposure. However, some of them may have resistance enough to live. Traces of pneumonia may be seen throughout the life of the birds, as there is a permanent injury to lung tissue.

Both animal and bird life have a means of making the best of lung injuries by completely sealing off the offending abscess. This later becomes a hard calcified mass. From this it can be seen that the area of functioning lung tissue is greatly reduced.

During cold, damp seasons, many young pheasants die from pneumonia. This is the easiest of all conditions to control, as it merely requires a constant regulation and watching of brooder temperature. During cold, damp spring weather, young birds get wet and do not dry out thoroughly and if exposed to drafts contract pneumonia.

3. Do Not Let Chicks Range on Ground Contaminated by Poultry. The pheasant is susceptible to many of the diseases and parasites of chickens and other poultry. Coccidia seem to be the chief offenders. The mortality is high, and the birds die within a week. This occurs mostly in birds from one to three weeks of age.

Although treatment now is relatively effective for both blackhead and coccidiosis, emphasis is placed on prevention rather than cure. General sanitation as to movements of coops, movements of brooder houses and runs in so far as it is possible is the recommended practice. Liming the soil followed by plowing or spading will help to decrease the infestation in the soil. However, after several generations of birds have used the same ground it can hardly be expected that disease and parasite free birds can be raised as successfully as on new ground.

4. **Feed and Water on Wire Frames and Disinfect Hoppers and Water Fountains Frequently.** This procedure is also essential as infected young birds will pass droppings into water and feed and expose the rest of the flock to parasites and diseases. The eggs of these parasites are not visible to the naked eye, and may be seen only by the aid of a microscope.

Hopper and water fountain disinfection is recommended as another very important step in the following of strict sanitary measures. Any chlorine disinfectant used around the farm for milk utensils will serve the purpose. The action of chlorine is powerful. It is the proper disinfectant to use because it has an affinity for hydrogen and separates the oxygen held by the water. Oxidation, of course, destroys organic matter. Bacteria and parasite eggs are either destroyed or injured to the extent that they no longer are active. No odor is left by the disinfectant during this process. This is quite important because birds may not eat foods that have offensive odors.

5. **Do not make sudden changes in the birds' ration.** This not only throws birds off feed but in some instances may result in long-term disturbance in nutrition.

6. **Remove the chill from all water given to chicks.** In the summer this can be done by the sun in a very few minutes. Keep a supply of fresh clean water before the chicks at all times.

7. **Provide plenty of shade and shelter.** Birds are more contented in cool shaded places especially during the hot weather months.

8. **Guard against cannibalism.** Cannibalism may develop during any stage in the life of young pheasants. However, the desire to dominate becomes more assertive in birds from two to three weeks of age. Should cannibalism occur during the first week of rearing, immediately check the temperature of the brooder to see that it is not too high. Supply more feeding hoppers and darken the brooder house windows. It would be advisable to keep succulent green foods before the birds constantly. Chopped cabbage, chopped lettuce, and chopped green alfalfa or other legumes are good sources of vitamin A. A lack of vitamin A is believed to be one of the causative factors.

Should cannibalism develop from the second to third week, allow the birds more range. It is advisable to construct roosts in the shelter pens. Small brush piles should also be added. Brooder house windows should also be darkened.

Should cannibalism develop after the third week, it can often be curbed by providing plenty of brush within the shelter pen so birds may escape from one another. Remove all picked birds and apply pine tar to the affected parts.

Do not attempt to rear birds of different ages in the same pen as this often induces the practice of cannibalism. It is recognized, however, that cannibalism or feather pulling is habit forming, and if it persists after the above preventatives have been carefully applied, debeaking may be the only sure cure. Debeaking can be applied after pheasants are three or four weeks old by removing the point from the upper beak. More information on this practice was given earlier in this book. An illustration showing a pheasant before and after debeaking follows.

Left—pheasant ready for debeaking to stop cannimalism or feather pulling. Right—pheasant after debeaking which removes the point from the upper beak.

To properly handle birds for debeaking, gently tuck the bird under your arm, exerting just enough pressure so it will not struggle. Place your hand around its breast with your thumb and forefinger holding the upper and lower beak together.

As you hold your bird, you will notice that there is a light line crossing over the top of the upper bill. You will notice that the line is fairly narrow over the top of the bill but widens out as it goes down to the side or edge of the bill. One method used is to start a cut by catching the blade of a sharp knife in the **edge** of the bill in the white line. **The cut should start two-thirds of the width of the white line towards the head.** If your cut starts on the front edge of the white line, you will not take off enough bill and it will grow out to soon. If you start your cut at the back edge of the white line, you will take off too much bill, and it will bleed.

After you catch the edge of your knife blade in the edge of the bill, using an upward and over motion, peel the front portion of the bill off leaving a portion of the quick (the darker portion of the beak) exposed. The quick is tender and care should be taken not to cut into the beak too far when you start, because then you will cut into the quick, which will cause considerable bleeding. This process should prevent the birds from picking for at least two weeks, and in severe cases of cannibalism, re-debeaking should take place at that time.

If you follow the few basic rules of management given in this chapter you should be able to successfully brood and rear pheasants without too much labor or expense.

Chapter IV

RAISING GROUSE, PARTRIDGE, AND QUAIL

The Gallinaceous or Upland Gamebirds are probably the most important order of birds to man. The common domesticated chicken is a prominent member of the group, which includes pheasants, turkeys, quail, and grouse. In all, there are 240 species of which eighteen are native to North America and were originally found in almost all habitats. Some have adapted quite well to changing conditions brought about by man and are holding their own or increasing. Others, such as the Heath Hen, a form of Prairie Chicken, have become extinct.

North American gallinaceous birds are grouped into three families. The first contains the grouse. The second family, made up of three subfamilies, encompasses quail, partridge, and pheasant. Turkeys form a third family of their own.

This book covered information on pheasants in the previous chapter. Grouse, partridge, and quail will be included in this section. Turkeys, because of their larger size and greater degree of domestication, will not be discussed in this book.

Grouse

Grouse are Northern Hemisphere birds with short, down-curved bills and feathered nostrils. Their legs are partly or completely feathered, and the toes of some are also feathered as a probable aid in walking on soft snow. Most have a bare colored patch over the eye. Males are larger than females and many have large, inflatable air sacs on the neck. Their food is chiefly leaves, buds, fruits, and some insects.

Common kinds of grouse include the following:

Blue Grouse	Sage Grouse
Greater Prairie Chicken	Sharp-Tailed Grouse
Lesser Prairie Chicken	Spruce Grouse
Ptarmigan	White-Tailed Ptarmigan
Rock Ptarmigan	Willow Ptarmigans
Ruffled Grouse	

This book will cover the rearing of grouse as a general group.

With some exceptions, grouse are considered fairly easy to raise. While their plumage is not as strikingly sensational and brightly colored as some others, they are endearing and interesting birds to raise. As with pheasants, following a few simple management rules, can make them a successful enterprise.

Mating Habits. Although kinds of grouse differ in spring breeding season behavior, the male grouse will usually put on quite a performance. As an example, the male Blue Grouse will get up on hollow logs to drum. He will "hoot" from a tall tree or from a ridge in areas where timber may be lacking. Hens will come to this hooting sound at mating time. They all seem to pick a favorite spot and continue to use this location. Male Prairie Chickens also gather on booming grounds in early spring for their courtship and mating. Each male has a territory of about thirty feet in diameter where he dances and "booms." The loud calls produced in the male is done by vibrating orange air sacs on the sides of his neck and can be heard at a distance of a mile or more. The males stamp their feet, erect their neck feathers, spread their tails, blow out their air sacs, and indulge in numerous battles with their neighbors. Mating gets underway at early dawn and lasts to mid-morning. A second performance is usually held in the late afternoon and continues on until nightfall. The hens cautiously approach the scene and quietly stroll about among the cocks until they make their mating choices.

In captivity grouse are fairly easy to raise and can be kept in pens similar to those used for other small game. It is not necessary to separate males from the females except when mating. Watch grouse very closely after mating, especially the Ruffled Grouse family. This male sometimes will kill the female after mating if they are not separated immediately. This problem is not generally severe with other kinds. Sometimes grouse will fight with their mates, but seldom fatally. It is recommended, however, that you watch all of them with more concern during the mating season.

Other species also have very interesting mating rituals which will not be covered here.

Grouse lay from eight to ten eggs. Blue Grouse usually lay fewer than the other kinds. The average clutch for Blue Grouse is around eight eggs and the incubation time is twenty-five to twenty-six days. As a contrast, Prairie Chickens lay about twelve eggs in a grass lined depression which take twenty-two to twenty-three days to hatch

Feeding. Most grouse like to peck on conifer trees located in their pens. If you can't raise these evergreen trees in pens, you may be able to cut fir and pine trees for this purpose. They should be tied to stand upright in the pens. Used Christmas trees are perfect for this purpose. In the winter time the grouse will eat the upper half of the fir needle. In the wild in the winter time, this is a primary source of food. Other feed which should be used include small grains (milo, cracked wheat, barley, cracked corn) and any kind of fruit, lettuce, cabbage, etc. Wild dandelions and any kinds of insects in the spring are also relished. Be sure the insects haven't been killed with a pesticide. Grouse do better on a variety of food and you will soon learn their particular preferences.

Meal worms are very helpful in raising grouse chicks which do not seem to want prepared feeds at various times. Some grouse raisers keep or buy a supply of meal worms for just this purpose. Most dealers in meal worms will include instructions on how to raise them when you buy stock. Turkey starter feeds are also recommended for young grouse chicks and should be fed as recommended in the chapter for pheasants.

Other Information and Management Practices. Prairie Chickens are the most delicate kind of grouse chicks to raise. This species formerly covered much of the open grasslands east of the Rocky Mountains in the prairie states. However, with the inroads of man, population, and necessary farm machinery, the Prairie Chicken is fast becoming almost extinct in all except a few areas. Most now seem to be concentrated in the sandy hills of Nebraska. There are a few other spot locations along the Mississippi River and the Canadian-Minnesota border. Because the specie is nearly extinct, it is practically impossible for private breeders to secure pairs of Prairie Chickens.

Management practices for raising other kinds of grouse are similar to raising pheasants. It is suggested that anyone interested in raising grouse read the chapter on pheasants, and others, in this book. As to basic practices, brooding, housing, feeding, and sanitation are for most purposes the same as for pheasants.

Proper Environment For Releasing Birds. In this connection it is only common sense that when releasing upland game birds to live under wild or open conditions, they be placed in areas similar to what they are accustomed to as native birds. Spacious areas where there are conifer spruce and juniper trees as well as grass, lagoons, and some grain fields will generally be suitable. Proper environment is very essential to their existence. Also, if they are fed at regular intervals, grouse, pheasants, and other small game birds will soon become dependent upon you to supply their food at all times. To make them look for food, they must have environment with natural foods in the wild. If natural food is not available, it may be necessary to plant shrubs, junipers, and some small grains before birds are released in any given area.

Partridge

Partridges are medium-sized old world birds that are plumper than quail. Their bills also lack the small projection or "tooth" serration found in quail. Both feet and legs are free of feathers on partridge. Two species have been introduced into North America from Eurasia and are reasonably well established. Chukar and Hungarian or gray Partridges are the kinds now found in the United States.

The Chukar is a native of dry south-eastern Europe and parts of Asia. Early attempts at introduction into the United States were failures. After repeated attempts, this bird is still not well established. They need semi-arid, open, rocky country and have consequently done best in parts of the West where adequate water is available. They are "handsome" birds, between quail and grouse in size, and easily recognized by their striking face pattern and barred flanks ("bib and tucker with striped waistcoat"). The Chukar has bold markings yet not conspicuous. The black eye-stripe runs down the neck and joins beneath the throat to form a "bib." Bright-red bill and feet, heavy black bars alongside the breast, and touches of rich chestnut on the crown tail, and underparts mark it a particular bird. It is extremely difficult to distinguish the male from the female as their markings are the same. They fly strongly, but, unless approached from above, prefer to escape by running uphill. During summer, they are seldom found far from water. The rest of the year they are widespread. As a rule, they are found in flocks of ten to forty birds. They prefer to roost on the ground, in the open or among rocks. In spring the birds pair off and, as soon as the eggs are laid in a hollow near a rock or bush, the males go off to form their own groups. The females incubate the creamy, brown-speckled eggs for twenty-one to twenty-two days. Later the males return and help care for the young chicks. Chukars feed mainly on weed seeds, wild fruits, leaves, and bulbs. The bulbs are dug out with their bills. Seasonal insects, especially grasshoppers, are important in their diet. The name of this bird comes from the sound of their call.

The Hungarian Partridge is a common European game bird which does well in habitats that will not support native species. It prefers a cool, somewhat dry climate and seems to thrive on open, cultivated lands in the north central states and adjacent Canada. Even in severe weather "Huns" can be found in the open searching for waste grain and weed seeds. Their gray breasts, chestnut belly patches, and short chestnut tails are good field marks.

Hungarian Partridges usually fly low and fast, alternating bursts of wing beats with coasting on stiffly arched wings. They move in winter in open areas in coveys of twenty to thirty birds.

In spring, the birds pair off with the males fighting continuously. Later each pair goes off to nest, making a shallow depression laid with grass or fine weeds. The female lays nine to twenty olive colored eggs which she incubates alone, like the Chukar, for about twenty-four days. She always covers the eggs with grass and leaves when she leaves the nest. The male stays nearby and later helps care for the young. This bird feeds primarily on grain gleaned from harvested fields. Wheat, barley, corn, oats, seeds of weeds and grasses, and some wild fruits are common food along with a few insects in the summer.

Raising Partridge In Captivity. For hatching and feeding partridge chicks and young poults, the same management practices mentioned previously for other wild game birds are practical.

In captivity, Hungarians lay five to twenty-five eggs with an average of sixteen eggs in a clutch. These are laid mostly during the first week of May. Old hens start nesting a week before young birds. Chukars start to lay eggs about mid-April to the first of May. A breeder can expect up to seventy to eighty eggs per bird if eggs are gathered on a daily routine.

Bantams and other hens recommended under the section for pheasants can be used to hatch partridge eggs but again it is suggested, that as soon as the brood hen has hatched out the young chicks, they be transferred to a brooder house by themselves for rearing.

Artificial brooding is done in small brooding houses equipped with electric brooders. Cotton seed hulls, shavings, or such materials should be used for litter. The general practices recommended for raising Chukar and Hungarian Partridge poults follow most of those previously discussed. Chukars, and sometimes Hungarian chicks, tend to crowd in large bunches into corners of pens or cages causing some to smother. Do not have square corners in your pens. Place extra wire or pieces of plywood to form rounded corners so chicks will not be able to crowd easily. The young should be kept on wire bottomed coops or on board-bottomed coops if the floor is covered with a good litter. Change this litter quite frequently.

Follow a regular game bird feeding program with partridge until they are ready for market or to be released. As the partridge's size is between the quail and pheasant so should his amount of feed. The partridge will be market size in about fourteen weeks. This fine bird is gaining the respect of many for its quality meat. They yield about sixteen ounces of the choicest all-white meat that can be obtained today. This bird is also gaining prominence in the sporting world. It is said that some hunters discuss him and others simply cuss him, but they are all fascinated by him. Anyone who has ever hunted partridge, especially the Chukar, will surely agree that this is one of the most "sporty" and difficult upland game birds to bag.

Quail

Quail are small to medium-size birds which have a single small projection or "tooth" on their bills. Their legs and feet are not feathered and the male has no spur. Male and female are approximately the same size. Quail are chicken-like, non-migratory birds. They are monogamous ground-nesters. Among the common kinds of quail found in the United States are the following:

Bobwhite Quail	Harlequin Quail
California Quail	Mountain Quail
Gambel's Quail	Scaled Quail

The Coturnix Quail has also been introduced into the U.S. but has not been successfully established.

The Bobwhite is probably the most popular gamebird even with those who do not hunt. If it has any competitor, it would be the Ring-Necked Pheasant. Because of the popularity of the Bobwhite, the following comprehensive information will be largely about this bird. What is said about the Bobwhite, however, generally also applies to the other kinds.

The Bobwhite Quail is a chunky small bird which becomes quite tame and often feeds near homes. Open pinewoods, brushy fields, abandoned farms, and similar habitats are preferred. A living fence of Multiflora Rose is excellent cover for them. Lespedeza is a good food crop. A dual planting of Multiflora Rose and Lespedeza is highly recommended.

Bobwhites usually travel on foot and stay in a quite limited area. For this reason, they need food and shelter close together.

Hedgerows and shelter belts encourage them in open areas. Most of the year they stay in coveys of a dozen or more birds. At night the covey will roost in a tight circle, heads out and tails in. This conserves heat in winter and permits fast getaway in case of danger. In spring, the covey breaks up. Males establish their territories and call the females with their loud and familiar "bobwhite." Pairs build nests on the ground in thick cover often in high grass. The nest is well made with an arch of woven grass over the top. Fourteen to sixteen white eggs hatch in about twenty-three days. Newly hatched birds are very small—thumb-sized—but grow rapidly and can fly in about two weeks. The males will help care for them. Bobwhites are almost omnivorous (eating all kinds of foods, plant and animal, indiscriminately). Leaves, buds, fruits, seeds, insects, and snails all find a place in their diet.

Selection of Breeders. The initial selection of breeding stock is the foundation of any successful quail rearing project. General physical condition is important in potential breeders. As with other game birds, choose the vigorous ones displaying good plumage and conformation. Generally breeders are not kept more than two breeding seasons, although birds will often lay surprisingly well the third and fourth seasons. Directly related cocks and hens should not be mated. By selecting individuals from the same geographic region, birds will already be adapted to the local climate. Since egg production is an important factor, stock should be selected from a source of birds with good laying records. In rearing your own breeders be sure to keep the earliest produced birds because they are generally the healthiest.

Fatalities. Land requirements will vary with the extent of the project. A back yard plot of 600 square yards would be sufficient for a hobby size operation capable of producing 500 quail annually. Sufficient space is extremely important for proper sanitation. Portable pens will need to be moved annually to new ground. In case of disease outbreaks, isolation areas may be necessary. In a commercial operation, twenty-five acres will be desirable for an annual production of 8,000 to 10,000 birds. A production site should be located that is convenient to the caretaker since it will be necessary to keep a close check on birds during such times as the early brooding part of the chick's life.

A great variety of breeding pens have been recommended and used throughout the country. For convenience and sanitary reasons, layers should be kept on one-half inch square welded wire, often referred to as hardware cloth. A brief modification of the layer cage, used by poultry farmers, has proved effective for quail. The individual pen is 12" x 20" x 10" with water and feed trays attached on the outside. A battery arrangement of these pens will accommodate twenty-four pair of quail in a two foot by six foot floor space. Smaller and less expensive pens are also available. Either automatic waterers or conventional watering trays can be used. A simple shed and windbreak should be provided for such a battery of caged layers. In the construction of pens it is advisable to use wire which is galvanized after weaving. The initial cost of this wire is slightly more; however, it lasts two to three times as long as wire galvanized before weaving. One inch is the largest mesh which is advisable. This size will exclude predators of the weasel group and starlings; each can be a costly nuisance during critical periods.

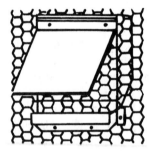 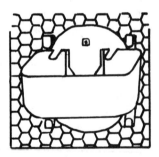

Feeder (left) and waterer (right) are designed to be filled from outside the pen to disturb the birds as little as possible.

Housing needs, other than shelters provided in individual pens, will consist of feed storage, incubator area, and brooder house. A basement or extra room will suffice for feed and incubator room for operations of less than 500 birds. However, brooder space will be necessary. A building twelve feet square will provide brooder space for an annual production of 500 birds if electrical brooders are used. If floor brooders are used the space should be increased slightly. The feed storage area must be kept dry. Housing for the brooders and incubators should be free of drafts but well ventilated. Incubators are most successful in an area such as a basement where fluctuating of relative humidity and temperature is at a minimum.

Equipment. Equipment can be rather simple or elaborate depending upon the size of the operation and financial investment. Information given here will favor the individual rearing small numbers of quail as a hobby, as opposed to the commercial enterprise.

Any type of trays, such as a rectangular bread pan, with a one inch layer of sand or small grain will serve to store eggs prior to incubation. As was explained earlier, a cool damp place is desirable to hold eggs. Equipment in which to store eggs is available but for a small operation the expense of elaborate egg holding facilities are not advisable. For a commercial operation egg holding equipment is highly recommended.

Circulating air incubators are generally considerably more efficient than still air incubating devices. Incubation is probably the most intricate step in quail production; therefore, it is extremely important to acquire good equipment for this part of the operation. Incubation with Bantams can be effective and was discussed in the chapter on pheasants.

Miscellaneous equipment will include such items as catching nets, transfer boxes, watering buckets, feed scoops, etc. A small meshed fish dip net serves well for catching birds. Well constructed conventional baby chick boxes suffice as shipping boxes. A small burlap bag will serve to transfer birds for short periods of time, provided birds are not overcrowded. All these items can be purchased at a local feed store or ordered from a farm supply house.

Supplies. Feed and medication supplies are generally available from a competent local poultry supply dealer. If possible, only feed prepared specifically for game birds should be used. Once a reliable dealer is selected, his recommended feeding program and supplies should be utilized without spasmotic changing to other sources. Application of medications should be limited to recommendations of competent dealers or veterinarians.

Care of Your Breeders. The introduction of "new blood" into a group of breeders is desirable but must be considered with

caution. To reduce the chances of introducing diseases or parasites, new stock should always be acquired from a disease free
source and held in quarantine for a month. If adult birds are
being used to introduce "new blood," by using only cocks you
reduce the chance of infesting stock with pullorum, since this
disease may be transferred from the hen to the chick via the
egg. Also egg production is more commonly affected when a
new source of hens are used. Introduction of "new blood" should
be necessary only about every three or four years.

Breeders should be paired off around mid-March. Locate the
breeder area in an isolated section where birds will not be
unnecessarily disturbed. A fence, around the entire production
and conditioning facility, capable of deterring stray dogs and
cats, is an excellent investment. Mate breeders with one hen to
one cock sex ratio for best fertility. Mating is occasionally un-
successful in one or more pairs of quail. In such a case the
cocks should be changed at once. If surplus hens are available,
total egg production can be increased by using a two hens to
one cock ratio. There is, however, likely to be an overall slight
decrease in egg fertility using this sex ratio. Breeding pens
should contain more than two square feet of floor space to accommodate three birds.

Egg production will begin in early April and continue
through August. Beginning when birds are mated in March, birds
should be fed a laying ration prepared by a reputable feed
dealer. The operator should try to use feed that is specifically
prepared for game birds and not a conventional poultry ration. Feed is provided in the dry form and kept before birds
at all times. Some laying rations are prepared containing grit
and oyster shells. These items should be kept before birds if
they are not included in the feed. Grain need not be fed during the laying season. If water is provided manually, a fresh
supply is necessary daily. A variety of feeders and waterers are
available from commercial sources. A dusting box is optional but
may not be necessary if birds are properly dusted for external
parasites prior to pairing. If a box is used, dry top soil and sand
should be kept one to three inches deep.

Care and Incubation of Quail Eggs. Eggs should be collected
daily and handled as little as possible. Place eggs in holding
trays, large end of eggs elevated slightly above small end, and

store in a cool place subject to the least possible amount of fluctuation in temperature. Ideally, eggs are held at temperatures of 55 to 65° F. When eggs are held at temperatures which range above 65° F. they should not be kept longer than one week before incubation. If production records are being kept on individual pairs, a soft lead pencil can be used to identify each egg with the producing pair.

The Bantam hen is an efficient mother of quail eggs for the small operator. With the recent improvements in small mechanical incubators, the use of Bantams has declined. However, by the operator who plans to rear less than a hundred quail, Bantams may be preferred. Since this type of incubation is declining in use, the technique will be only briefly described. Depending on the size of the operation, the initial cost of Bantam hens and cost of nest boxes will very likely be more expensive than a low priced incubator capable of doing the same job.

Healthy, disease and parasite-free hens should be selected for incubating eggs. Lightweight Bantams of one of the smooth leg breeds are preferred. Use an enclosed nest box approximately 12" x 12" x 12" attached to a 36" x 12" x 12" wire covered run for feeding, watering, and exercise. Place the broody hen in the nest box but release her into the run once daily. If she does not willingly return to the nest, which is prepared with dry grass and dummy eggs, then put her back after about 15 minutes. When the hen has become sincere at incubating the eggs, then the dummy eggs can be replaced with a clutch of sixteen to twenty good quail eggs. Allow the hen off the nest fifteen to twenty minutes daily throughout the incubation period. When the chicks are hatched and dry, they should be removed to artificial brooders.

Mechanical incubators vary widely in cost. Circulating types generally give the best performance; however, the still air models are less expensive and will give acceptable performance for small number of eggs. In purchasing an incubator it is important that an operator anticipate his future need and acquire a sufficiently large and good quality unit. If there is an anticipated need for incubation of more than 200 quail eggs at one time, it is advisable to go to one of the circulating air models. It is extremely important that the manufacturer's directions be closely followed. A continuous temperature and humidity level makes it necessary that an attendant check incubator controls and indicators every few hours throughout incubation. At the beginning of each season the incubator should be run for a test period prior to setting eggs.

The incubator should be located where temperature and relative humidity ranges fluctuate very little and out of areas frequented by drafts and periods of direct sunlight. Often a basement proves an ideal site.

There are general rules which may be helpful in incubation, although specific directions may vary between types of incubators. If these rules are contrary to the manufacturer's directions, then the latter should be followed. It should be noted whether manufacturer's instructions are for game birds or solely for domestic chickens. The temperature range in still air incubators, for the first sixteen days, is between 101 and 102° F. The last seven days it should be increased by approximately $\frac{1}{2}$° F. A humidity level of 55 to 65 per cent is recommended until eggs begin pipping when it should be raised to about 75 per cent. For circulating air incubators, temperature for the first twenty days is between 99½ and 100° F. The humidity for this period is maintained at 80 per cent as determined by a hygrometer. Three days prior to hatching, the temperature is raised one degree and just before pipping the humidity is increased to 90 per cent. Humidity in the incubator is controlled by the rate of evaporation. This rate is determined by the surface area of water in the incubator. Water trays and instructions are provided with each type of incubator. In dry weather the humidity can be increased by sprinkling eggs or putting water soaked sponges in the egg trays. It is important not to open the incubator door any more than is necessary during hatching. This will keep humidity from fluctuating.

Eggs should be turned a minimum of three times daily during the first twenty days of incubation. Turning should not be practiced during the last three days. It is important that eggs be turned and turning be an odd number of times daily. This insures against eggs being left in the same position night after night. If an automatic turning device is used, studies have indicated that turning eggs every three or four hours increases hatchability slightly.

Fumigation of eggs during incubation, or prior to incubation, is an effective control of pullorum and mushy-chick disease. The potassium permanganate-formalin technique is the most commonly used method. Fumigation instructions of the incubator manufacturer, advice from local competent hatchery operators, or state university poultry department assistance should be sought before undertaking this procedure. With strict incubation and hatching sanitation, extensive fumigation procedures will not generally be necessary.

After chicks are hatched, they should be left in the incubator until completely dry. This period may be overnight without damage to chicks. Chicks should be carried to pre-warmed brooders in a warm, cloth-lined box to prevent chilling.

Eggs may be tested or candled on the twentieth day as they are moved to the hatching compartments of the incubator. This allows the elimination of spoiled eggs which might burst and cause a bad odor in the trays. Candling is accomplished with a light in the same manner as with chicken eggs.

Brooding and Rearing Management. The more recently developed electrical brooding units are suitable for brooding and growing birds. Such a unit, is equipped with controls, a heating system, and the necessary area to rear seventy-five birds simultaneously to five weeks of age. Only conventional chick waterers and feeders need be added. These units can be stacked in battery fashion for ease of handling and saving of space. If more than 500 quail are produced annually, most operators prefer to use floor brooders. In order to verify proper operation of brooders, units should be operated several hours prior to receiving chicks. Brooding directly on the floor makes easier handling of larger quantities of birds. Infra-red lamps may be used; however, the consumption rate of electricity is considerably more than with the floor hover-type brooder. If this lamp is used it should be kept at least eighteen inches off the floor. In floor brooding a circular guard of one foot high wire, six to ten feet in diameter, is placed around the brooder. This guard can be removed after four or five days or when chicks have learned where to find heat, food, and water. Floor space requirements are nine chicks per square foot for chicks up to ten days old and six chicks per square foot up to six weeks of age. One half inch of linear feeding space per chick is re-

quired for chicks up to ten days old. This amount is doubled
for birds up to six weeks of age. One linear foot of watering
space is sufficient for starting 100 chicks. This amount should
be doubled after ten days. Fresh, clean water and dry feed are
kept before growing birds. To start chicks eating, it is sometimes necessary to sprinkle feed before birds on a white paper
towel or cloth. This is recommended in the immediate vicinity
of the feeder. As chicks begin eating from the paper, small
amounts can be raked from the feeder and around its edges
to encourage use of the feeder. If birds are brooded on the
floor a litter of materials such as shavings, peanut hulls, ground
corn cobs, crushed cornstalks, or sugar cane pumis can be used.
The litter must be kept dry and clean. In order to eliminate
unsanitary conditions, feeder and watering areas are raised two
to four inches above the littered floor on a section covered
with one-half inch hardware cloth. It may be necessary to set
feeders and waterers directly on litter near the brooder the
first few days until birds become accustomed to the area.

Maintain a temperature of 90 to 100° F. for the first week.
The temperature should then be lowered at the rate of 5° F.
per week. Heat may not be required after $3\frac{1}{2}$ to $4\frac{1}{2}$ weeks,
depending on the outside temperature. Temperature readings
should be taken at litter level and at the warmest point to
which chicks have access.

Cannibalism can be effectively controlled by not overcrowding, control of ventilation, control of light, and debeaking.
Darkening of growing area will often control feather picking.
It is important to maintain adequate ventilation, especially during hot weather when temperatures are fluctuating within a
wide range. Chicks may be debeaked when 1 day old by using
finger nail clippers to trim the horny end of the upper beak
back to the pink portion. Birds will probably need debeaking
again at six and twelve to fifteen weeks of age. Electric de-
beakers are available for handling large numbers of birds. This
procedure cauterizes the beak. Care should be taken not to
cut off too much beak or to cut the tongue in debeaking. The
degree of debeaking necessary will depend upon the degree of
cannibalism experienced.

After birds have been kept in brooders for about one week
without heat, (when they are five to six weeks of age) trans-

fer can be made to growing and conditioning pens. The change from starter feed is made to a grower ration at the time of transfer from brooders to conditioning pens. Transfer boxes do an adequate job for this move. This is a critical change and birds should be watched closely for the first few days. If weather is unseasonably cool the transfer is best delayed a few days. In the case of a sudden rain during the first few days following transfer, it may be necessary to return birds to heated brooders to dry off. Mortalities at this period can be severe, from piling and suffocation of birds, due to wet, cool weather. Birds are kept in conditioning pens until time for selling or release. These pens also serve as ideal holding pens for retaining breeders until pairing off in March.

Other Management Practices. Diseases in quail propagation sometimes can be a real problem. The practice of "common sense" can alleviate many so called complicated problems. Often, you must turn to poultry diagnostic specialists for assistance. It is necessary that the operator become acquainted with poultry disease specialists in his area. The caretaker must keep alert to early symptoms of morbidity. Early treatment with present day poultry drugs is usually quite effective in controlling complications. There is no treatment substitute for strict sanitation throughout the entire quail operation. The operator will reap dividends with a minimum of effort if sanitation is practiced.

Disposing of dead birds is important in operations of any size. Small production units can accomplish this by burning or burying carcasses with little effort. All remains of carcasses should be completely burned or buried out of the reach of dogs and rodents. The larger producer should consider a disposal pit like those used on poultry farms. Instructions for construction of such a pit are available from poultry departments of state universities.

The temperament in which a caretaker handles birds is important. Movements in and near pens should be steady and continuous and not spasmodic and swift. Sudden and sharp noises should be kept to a minimum. Birds will become used to a caretaker or the general type of clothing worn. This will reduce pen injuries. Birds should not be handled while their plumage is wet as this will result in considerable loss of feathers. In shipment, birds should be provided with good ventilation. Water and feed is not necessary for the first two days of shipment.

Conditioning the Birds. The methods of properly conditioning birds vary with the purpose for which they are being reared.

Quail raised for meat production can be reared in cages of any size. These birds do not need as much space as those being conditioned for release. Large numbers of birds can be reared together if cannibalism is controlled. Cages should be located where they will be dry, well ventilated and convenient for the caretaker. Water and proper game bird feed should be available at all times. When birds are being reared for meat, it is best if they do not retain wild characteristics.

Birds for exhibits can also be reared in cages of any size but the number in each cage should be small. All possible measures should be taken to prevent these birds from pecking, fighting, or becoming exicted and flying into sides of cages. Location of pens and feeding programs are the same as for birds being reared for meat. The physical appearance of these birds is most important. They should be full-plumaged and have a healthy appearance.

Birds released for hunting require different treatment. Two techniques are presently being used.

Conditioning birds begins when they are placed in brooder units as chicks. Constant exposure to humans and animals tends to tame them. No one should be allowed in the brooding and holding area except the caretaker. Keeping people and dogs away from birds is believed more important than the type of pens in which they are reared. Birds are normally moved into conditioning pens at five or six weeks of age, depending on the weather. At this point, the methods of conditioning vary. Some persons prefer large flight pens and others use relatively small conditioning pens. Quail can be properly conditioned and mature enough to release in the field when they are seventeen to eighteen weeks old.

Flight pens are large enough to (1) permit quail to develop their flying abilities, (2) to condition them to weather and (3) allow them to become accustomed to being on the ground prior to being released afield. Such a pen is about twelve feet wide, 130 feet long and 6½ feet tall. It will hold approximately

1,000 quail (1.5 sq. ft. per bird). The flight pen and propagation facility should consist of a brooder house and sun porch for young birds and a flight pen for older birds. Some operators have brooder houses located in areas separate from flight pens to help prevent spread of disease.

Sides and top of the flight pen are completely covered with poultry wire. The ground may serve as the bottom on well drained sites or one-half inch hardware cloth may be used. The base of the wire (about one foot) on the sides of the pens is bent outward to a 90 degree angle, placed in a plowed furrow and covered with dirt. This discourages predators which might attempt to dig into the pens. The sides and top should not be stretched tight. The wire needs to be slightly loose to reduce the shock for birds flying into it.

Pens should be built on isolated locations where vegetation is quite thick. Trees, bushes and tall weeds should be left standing around the pen to provide natural surroundings and prevent birds from observing things which may tend to tame them. If natural vegetation is sparse, some tall growing plants such as corn or giant sorghum varieties should be planted.

Proper vegetation should also be left standing within the pen area. This vegetation should be thick enough to provide hiding places for birds but thin enough to allow sunlight to penetrate to keep the area dry and act as a sanitizing agent. Small woody brush in one section of the pen is especially valuable as cover. Tall, large stalked weeds also provide good cover. Grasses are not good cover and they mat up on the ground and cause areas to stay damp. Natural vegetation usually doesn't last more than one season because large numbers of birds trample it down.

Before placing birds in pens the second year, a few rows of thick stalked plants such as grain sorghum and dwarf corn should be established to provide cover. Pens should never be without adequate cover. If quail become accustomed to open areas while in conditioning pens, they will seek the same type areas when released. Brushy cover should be established if herbaceous vegetation becomes trampled down. Small pine and cedar trees stacked in pens make good cover.

Waterers and feeders should be at each end and in the middle of pens. This helps keep birds from congregating. Large, outdoor-type-feeders should be used which will not need refilling often. Additional waterers and feeders should be kept. By taking filled containers into pens and bringing empties out, a caretaker can make fewer trips into pens and remain for shorter periods. Waterers and feeders should be relocated when an area becomes wet or messy with spilled water and feed. Commercial feed should be supplemented with whole grains such as heads of millet, wheat, grain sorghum, sunflower or other foods planted on the shooting area.

Pens should be examined daily for sick or dead birds and unsanitary conditions. Immediate measures should be taken to correct these conditions. Disease spreads rapidly where large numbers of birds are congregated, especially when pens are wet and covered with bird droppings. Medication produced by reputable manufacturers will prevent many disease problems. Instructions should be carefully followed when using medications.

A second method of conditioning birds for release is relatively new. The theory behind this method is that quail do not need large flight pens to become good fliers. It is believed that allowing the birds to become conditioned to weather and grain foods on isolated areas is most important. Birds are reared in brooders until they are six weeks old, when they are transferred to conditioning pens. Conditioning pens are smaller and may be less expensive for persons handling smaller numbers of birds. Such a pen is about 28 feet long, 8 feet wide, 3 feet high and stands on legs 3 feet tall. The sides and top can be one inch poultry wire and the bottom is one-half inch hardware cloth. A pen this size holds 100 quail with little danger of cannibalism. One end of the pen is a shelter area and a sun porch is on the other end; both are about 3 feet wide. Pens similar to these but without hardware cloth floors and legs may be used but must be located on well drained areas. If pens are placed on the ground, the top and sides should be made of one-quarter inch hardware cloth. Wire on the sides should extend under the ground about ten inches to prevent rats from getting into the pens and eating the bird feed.

Conditioning pens are also placed in isolated locations where vegetation is thick. Small tree limbs or bushes should be laid on top of the cages for overhead cover. This tends to make birds seek cover when released. Small pines or cedar trees can be placed in corners of these cages to serve as cover. Only one caretaker should tend the birds.

Feeding programs should be the same in both of the methods described. Using either of these methods, birds can be conditioned and ready for the field in ten to twelve weeks if they are placed in the pens when six weeks old.

Releasing The Birds. Methods of releasing pen-reared quail vary with the purpose for which they are being released. Some operators release small numbers of quail and hunt them within two hours; others release large numbers several weeks or months before hunting them; still others release pairs of quail in the Spring hoping they will rear coveys. Results of these releases depend largely on how well birds are conditioned prior to release and the condition of the habitat in which they are released. Birds which are not strong, healthy fliers and have not been conditioned to food and weather will soon succumb to disease, predators and bad weather. Even well conditioned birds cannot survive on a poor range. So, properly managed habitat is just as important as having healthy, well conditioned birds, unless you plan to release and shoot them the same day.

When quail are released for immediate hunting they are removed from conditioning pens and placed in small wire release cages for transporting to the field. Release cages should be small so birds cannot move freely. They may injure themselves or become exhausted if placed in large cages. A small wire basket-type release cage can be made of one-inch poulty wire. The cage size may vary but should be only large enough to hold the birds you plan to release at one location. A cage approximately ten inches wide, ten inches long and three and one-half inches tall will hold six quail. A door is located at one end of the cage. Several cages should be made so birds can be released simultaneously at several locations. After birds are placed in release cages, the cages should be covered with a burlap sack. In this manner the cage is darkened and the quail are unable to see the handlers. This keeps birds calm and still permits adequate ventilation. Birds should be placed in the cage an hour or two prior to being released to allow them time to recover from the shock of being handled.

At release sites, cages are placed in good cover. A small amount of grass should be bent over the cage. Thick vegetation should not be immediately in front of the cage opening because it may cause the quail to remain in the cage. Cages are placed with ends opening towards the person making the releases. This prevents birds from immediately running out. The person making the release opens the cage and slowly moves away from the area. Birds normally move out of the cages in ten to thirty minutes. After thirty to forty minutes the birds may be hunted. By this time properly conditioned birds are normally settled and provide good shooting. An average recovery of 70 percent can be expected with this type release. However, this depends on the condition of the birds, the shooting area and the abilities of dogs and hunters.

Quail released five to eight weeks prior to hunting have sufficient time to become adapted to the "wild" and normally react just like their wild cousins. However, since these birds will be in the field for a long time prior to hunting, many will never be recovered. Approximately twenty to thirty-five percent recovery is the best that can be expected.

Releasing techniques differ greatly when birds are stocked several weeks in advance of hunting. Stocking is the most critical adaptation period in the lives of pen-reared birds and careful attention to habitat development and releasing methods is essential. These birds should be given every opportunity to become adapted to the "wild" if expected to survive the many natural enemies they will face when released.

The "gentle" release method provides best results when stocking birds several weeks prior to hunting. Gentle release pens may be built in various sizes and shapes. One which is practical, easily built, and is easy to transport has framing of 1 x 4 inch lumber. Eighteen gauge, one-inch poultry wire is used to cover the pen. It is made so it can easily be disassembled and moved. Pens consist of two sides nine feet long and six feet from base to top and two end sections. Three hinges hold the top together and allow the sides to fold together for moving or storing. Ends are separate and bolted to the sides. Doors are at each end. One foot of wire extends outward from the base boards. This is covered with dirt to keep predators out. This cage is suitable for twenty quail.

Pen-reared quail retain many of their natural instincts and because of this, careful consideration has to be given to any stocking program. One instinct retained to some degree is not to tolerate over-crowding. One pen (twenty birds) for fifteen acres of intensively managed range is about maximum. On areas without an abundance of properly distributed food and cover, the number of b:rds released per acre will have to be less.

The release of quail long in advance of hunting must be made on good quail range. If an area cannot support wild quail it will certainly not support pen-reared ones. Any attempt to stock quail on poor range will be a waste of time, money and effort. These releases are usually made on areas where quail populations are low due to over shooting or a poor nesting season.

Gentle release pens should be placed in the field several days prior to releasing birds in them. They should be placed on well drained areas near good cover and food. Feeders and waterers should be filled and placed in the cages under some brush. Grain harvested from shooting area plots should be scattered in the pens.

FIELD BORDER STRIP

Quail approximately eight weeks of age or older are ready to be removed from conditioning pens and placed in gentle release pens.

The pens should be checked daily and food and water added as needed. Birds should remain in these pens seven to ten days. Releases should be made early in the morning on a day when good weather is forecast. This allows birds approximately ten hours of daylight to become familiar with their new range.

To release birds, open the door of the cage near good vegetative cover. Walk slowly to the opposite end and allow the quail to walk out rather than fly.

Pens can be moved if needed for additional releases. If pens are not needed, the door can be closed after one bird is placed in the pen as a "call bird". This lonesome bird will call often and tends to keep the released covey near the pen. "Call birds" are particularly valuable when coveys are scattered by predators. Pens left on the site should have the doors closed to prevent birds from re-entering and becoming trapped by predators.

Feed and water should be available in containers, like those the birds have been using and should be placed on release areas for approximately two weeks. This provides birds with abundant familiar food while they learn to find natural foods. When this gentle release method is used, birds should be released at least three weeks prior to hunting and they should be at least sixteen weeks old before they are hunted.

Another gentle release method used by some large operators involves less labor and expense. However, end results may not be as good as the technique previously discussed. Major differences in the two methods is size of release pens and length of time birds remain in them.

Pens used are two feet long, two feet wide and fives inches tall. Tops are covered with tin. Sides and bottoms are one-half inch hardware cloth. Ends are made of wood. Water and food containers are attached on the insides, to the end pieces. Each pen holds twenty birds.

When the quail are 9 weeks of age or older they are removed from the conditioning pens and placed immediately in release pens. They are carried to the field in release pens. Pens are then hung on a wooden tripod or tree limb situated near good food and cover. Food and water containers like those used in conditioning pens are placed nearby. Birds remain in release pens overnight. Early the following morning, pen doors are opened and the caretaker slowly moves away. Birds are permitted to move out when they desire. A few hours later, after all birds have left the pens, a "call bird" is placed in the release pen. "Call birds" are released about three weeks later when coveys become familiar with their range.

Spring releases of paired quail are made by some operators in hopes that the birds will rear young. These releases are of questionable value. Definite proof that released pairs have any appreciable influence on increasing quail populations is sparse. Information of this nature has been difficult to collect. The effect of these releases may depend on (1) the number of native quail present on the area; (2) conditions of the range; (3) condition of released pairs; (4) predator population on the area; and (5) weather conditions during the nesting season.

If the range is in good condition and enough quail survive the winter, there may be no need to release pairs. However, if the range is in good condition and the quail population was "over-shot" then fair results may be possible.

The comprehensive coverage of quail in this chapter should make it easier to raise this popular game bird with a greater degree of success. Much of the information presented, especially on conditioning and releasing of birds, also applies to other upland game species included in this book.

Chapter V

WATERFOWL
MANAGEMENT

Ducks, geese, and swans make up the waterfowl (family Anatidae). There are over 200 species. Forty-five are native to North America. This book will consider ducks and geese, with the major emphasis on ducks since they are most commonly raised as game birds.

From our earliest times, ducks and geese have been important to man as a source of food and, more recently, for sport. Their down and feathers have stuffed many a pillow and comforter, and still are used to some extent for that purpose. Goose quills were the "ball-point pens" of centuries gone by. Waterfowl also give much pleasure to millions who watch and study their habits as well as to sportsmen who hunt them.

All waterfowl share certain characteristics which affirm their relationship. Some of these are: (1) Bills flattened to some degree with small, tooth-like edges; (2) Four toes on each foot three webbed and the fourth small and free (see illustration); (3) Legs short, set wide apart, making them "waddle" in their land walk; (4) Dense feathers over a heavy layer of down; (5) Waterfowl moult all of their flight feathers at once, and are therefore flightless for a period of time each year.

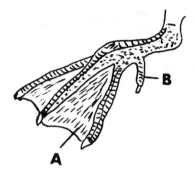

Duck Foot—A is webb connecting three toes. B shows the fourth small free toe.

Waterfowl must have wetlands. With the draining of marshlands for intensive cropping, careful planning will be required to save these birds for the future.

Ducks may be classified into groups. Two such classifications are River Ducks and Sea Ducks. With both kinds, the sexes differ in color and the bill is broad and flattened. They differ in other characteristics.

River Ducks have a small hind toe without a lobe or flap; their legs are near the center of the body; and they feed by "tipping up" mainly on plant food. In taking flight, River Ducks spring directly up with a single bound.

Sea Ducks have a hind toe with a flap or lobe; feed by diving after fish, shellfish, and some marine plants; and in taking flight run along the water. Sea Ducks have short legs, set well back on their body, and are excellent swimmers.

Common kinds of River and Sea Ducks include the following:

River Ducks

American Widgeon	Gadwall	Mottled Duck
Black Duck	Green-Winged Teal	Pintail
Blue-Winged Teal	Mallard	Ruddy Duck
Cinnamon Teal	Masked Duck	Shoveller
European Widgeon	Mexican Duck	Wood Duck

Sea Ducks

Barrow's Goldeneye	Greater Scaup	Ring-Necked Duck
Bufflehead	Harlequin Duck	Spectacled Eider
Canvasback	King Eider	Steller's Eider
Common Eider	Lesser Scaup	Surf Scoter
Common Goldeneye	Oldsquaw	White-Winged Scoter
Common Scoter	Redhead	

The information given in this book will center mainly around the Mallard. Mallards are the most important ducks to man, being the ancestor of nearly all domestic forms which are prized for their feathers, flesh, and eggs. For the same reasons, they are a very popular game bird. They are large ducks, excellent for eating and prized by hunters.

Geese have necks longer than ducks; the sexes are alike in color; bills are high, not flattened; they feed on land and in water by "tipping up;" and in taking flight rise after a short run.

Kinds of geese include the following:

American Brant	Emperor Goose
Black Brant	Snow Goose
Blue Goose	White-Fronted Goose
Canada Goose	

The Canada Goose is the best known and most widely distributed. There are few places where one of the subspecies cannot be seen at some season of the year. Common subspecies are Common, Western, and Lesser Canada geese, and Richardson's and Cackling geese. All are similarly marked and vary principally in size and darkness of coloration. Flocks migrating north are hailed as harbingers of spring and their trip south as prophets of winter. On shorter flights to and from feeding grounds the flocks seldom assume the familiar V-shape of migration flight, but move in irregular groups. Many small flocks are distinct families, for geese mate for life and family ties are strong. The old gander (male) usually leads on migration and is believed to teach the young the route. Migratory habits of geese have been watched and studied by man for years and yet we still know little about them.

Most geese nest on the ground, but occasionally nest on cliffs. The female incubates five or six dull, creamy white eggs. The gander stands by for protection and helps rear the brood. Canada Geese are known for their high degree of intelligence and often hide to avoid detection. They feed on land, grazing on young plants and picking up waste grain. Their size and wariness have made them a prime favorite with sportsmen and raisers of game birds.

Snow geese are probably the most abundant of our geese but are limited largely to coastal areas. The Blue Goose is the most distinctive North American goose but again can only be found in a limited number of regions. Materials in this chapter will be most applicable to the Canada Goose because of its widespread adaptability and popularity with hunters and game raisers.

Habitat Management For Raising Ducks In Open Areas

Landowners can make their wetlands support more waterfowl by adopting a few well-proved management practices. Wetland can be valuable duck habitat and general suggestions are made in this chapter for that use.

Knowing the kinds of food that ducks like will help develop a clear understanding of attractive habitat. The foods ducks prefer are found by examining gizzard contents. In a recent Missouri study, 2,252 gizzards from seventeen kinds of ducks gathered in that state during the fall hunting season were examined. The following six foods were the most important by amounts eaten:

1.	Corn	22%
2.	Smartweeds	20%
3.	Wild millet	17%
4.	Acorns	9%
5.	Cutgrass	5%
6.	Chufa	2%
		75%

Many other foods were eaten, but these six kinds comprised three-fourths of the total volume.

The occurrence rate of foods indicates their availability and attractiveness. The foods which appeared most frequently in the 2,252 gizzards examined were:

1.	Smartweeds	73%
2.	Wild millet	41%
3.	Bulrushes	26%
4.	Cutgrass	19%
5.	Corn	19%
6.	Pondweeds	11%
7.	Chufa	10%
8.	Spike-rushes	10%
9.	Acorns	9%

The high rating of smartweeds and wild millet as fall foods for ducks in both tables is important. It shows they provide a substantial amount of food, and are liked by most kinds of ducks.

The smartweeds and wild millet thrive in fertile, moist soils commonly found in the bottomlands of streams. All species of ducks eat millet and smartweed seeds, but shoal water feeders such as mallards, pintails, shovelers and teal seem to be especially fond of them.

Acorns are an important high energy food for mallards and wood ducks. When available, they are one of the choicest foods of both species. Other ducks eat acorns, but most of them only occasionally.

Agricultural crops, particularly corn, are attractive to mallards. Pintails and green-winged teal occasionally feed in dry corn fields that have been harvested, but greatest use by all species of dabbling ducks comes when these fields are flooded. Waste grain is eagerly fed upon, but weed seeds are also highly important. Ragweeds, foxtails, pigweeds, millet and smartweeds are generally common in corn, soybean and milo fields, and their seeds are relished by ducks. Flooding makes them readily available.

A number of marsh plants develop seeds or other parts attractive to ducks. Luxurious beds of rice cutgrass developed on the rich, moist soils in the bottomlands and marshes which dry late in the growing season. It can withstand severe flooding. Ducks eat the seeds and, to a lesser degree, the roots.

Where it grows, Chufa also produces a highly attractive duck food. This plant thrives on lowlands subject to periodic floodings. Underground nutlets are produced as the soil dries in late summer, and these are relished by ducks.

Other marsh plants, such as the bulrushes, pondweeds, and spike-rushes, produce duck foods. They occur naturally in most permanent marches.

There is little indication that ducks have seasonal preferences for certain foods. The food's availability appears to be far more important. An example of this is the use of flooded agricultural land by many species of ducks. Farm ponds offer another example. They are usually low in late summer, and the slowly exposed mudflats often develop fine stands of attractive foods which are ignored by ducks in the fall. When filled by winter run-off, these ponds become attractive to migrating ducks in the spring, partly because the food crops have been flooded. Wood ducks will search for acorns on the dry forest floor, but for all practical purposes timber stands must be flooded before acorns get the best use.

Ducks like water, and they prefer to feed there. The wise wetland manager interested in duck hunting will arrange to have an abundance of duck foods made available by shallow flooding.

Ducks use a wide variety of aquatic habitats. The kind occupied is often governed by the availability of food and sanctuary. Some species, such as canvasback and redheads, have rather specific habitat preferences. Others, such as the mallard, are opportunists and use all kinds of wetlands.

Marshes. Marsh land is an important habitat for ducks. Marshes may be defined as low-lying tracts of level land which are more or less permanently flooded, and vegetated to a variable degree by water-tolerant plants. The kind of plants is influenced by the season of flooding and drying, depth and permanence of water, turbidity, bottom soil type, water chemistry, animal life, and even by the size and shape of the marsh. Marshes with a high percentage of emergent vegetation are preferred by mallards, pintails, shovelers, teal, baldpate, gadwall, and other puddle ducks. Those with large expanses of open or nearly open water are frequented by canvasback, redheads, scaup and ruddy ducks—the divers.

Marshes in the northern prairies of the United States and Canada are used for breeding purposes by almost all species of common ducks. They provide the food, cover, loafing areas, and brood rearing habitat needed by nesting ducks.

Flooded Timber. Shallowly flooded timber is attractive to mallards and wood ducks. It is unusual to find other species using this habitat. Mallards and wood ducks are, however, two very important species to duck hunters. While pin and willow oak stands are preferred because of their food supply, mallards and wood ducks will use any kind of flooded timber for cover, if not for feeding.

Timber stands can be flooded safely when trees are dormant, but flooding during the growing season will eventually kill all but a few species.

Ponds. Farm ponds are used by ducks mostly during the spring migration. Food availability has already been discussed, but disturbance and duck behavior are also important factors. Ponds are hunted in the fall, and their small size and scattered location greatly reduces their attractiveness as sanctuaries. Also, in the fall and winter ducks seek others of their kind and gather into conspicuous flocks. In spring, they are interested in forming pairs, and they become less tolerant of their fellows. Pairs or small groups of several species are commonly found on farm ponds in the spring.

Ponds differ from marshes in several ways. Ponds are deeper, usually support fish life, are usually free of emergent vegetation, and receive more use by livestock and humans. Consequently they are less attractive to ducks.

Lakes. Migrating and wintering ducks often use large lakes for loafing and roosting. Most lakes offer sanctuary only, and ducks using them feed in neighboring fields. Some lakes attract diving ducks that feed on submerged aquatic vegetation, shell fishes, snails, and small fish.

Rivers. Rivers, in some cases, can provide a suitable habitat for ducks. In some areas they are an important part of the migration route. Old river "oxbows" and cutoffs provide marsh-type habitat in a basically river environment. They are especially suitable if they contain or are close to a good food source.

The management of aquatic habitat can be quite challenging, and it is helpful if certain guide lines are recognized.

Water Depth. Dabbling ducks successfully feed in water ranging up to 18 inches in depth, but seldom use the bottom foods in deeper water. Excessive depths may also be an expensive waste of water, particularly if it is pumped.

Flooding. If adequate water control is available and the supply is unquestioned, it is wise to delay flooding until shortly before the earliest fall migrants are expected. Some seeds, particularly millet, deteriorate under water, and early flooding in warm weather hastens this process. An exception to this suggestion would be made if blackbirds are a problem. Early flooding is one way to help reduce millet losses if large flocks of these birds appear. When the variation in topography exceeds 18 inches, controlled progressive flooding can make new feeding area available over an extended period of time.

Draw-down. In areas that are heavily shot, draw-down should be started at the close of the duck season. Spent lead pellets are readily consumed by feeding ducks that mistake them for gravel. These pellets are ground in the gizzard, and lead poisoning may result. This malady usually is fatal, or at best weakens the bird and increases his vulnerability to predators, diseases and parasites. Over-filling to remove lead from the reach of birds is as effective as draw-down, provided water depths in the potential feeding areas exceed 24 inches, and geese or diving ducks are not present.

Cultivation is useful to reduce lead contamination. The heavy pellets tend to sink into the loosened soil and eventually settle out of the reach of feeding ducks.

If an adequate supply of water is available, controlled draw-down can be an effective way to acquire at low cost, stands of wild millet and smartweeds. The timing of draw-down, and the species of plants which naturally result, varies, but the principles are as follows:

1) Hold water on the land until early summer. This will discourage undesirable plants which need dry land to germinate.
2) Drain the land in late June or early July to expose the bottom. Early draining favors wild millet, and delayed draining favors the smartweeds.
3) If there is any question about the natural seed supply, sow the wet soil immediately with wild or domesticated millet.

When summer rainfall is deficient and the soil becomes excessively dry, irrigation may become necessary. Millet and smartweeds will tolerate brief periods of flooding. Indeed, they often grow in shallow water.

Weed Control. Most natural duck food plants thrive on rich, moist soils of alluvial origin. Some, like millet, are poor competitors for light, nutrients and moisture. They gain their dominance because growing conditions, particularly at the early stages, are unfavorable for other plants. Japanese millet is a good domesticated variety for direct planting on managed areas. It is a poor competitor, and sometimes needs a bit of help from the manager. Broadleaved rivals such as cockleburr and morning glory can be discouraged with herbicides. The need for such treatment should be compelling, however, because the same spray will also destroy valuable broad-leaved food plants such as the smartweeds.

Fertilization. The value of fertilizing marshland is debatable. Marshes usually occur on basically rich soils, and they are frequently rejuvenated by periodic flooding and drying. Moisture, rather than fertility, is more often a critical factor limiting plant growth in marshes. Artificial marshes of course may be created on soil types with varying levels of fertility. Under these circumstances, chemical fertilization to increase seed production may well be worthwhile.

Forest Management. The food base of virtually all woodlands managed for ducks can be improved. Non-mast-producing trees and understory species can be removed, and the resulting openings planted to suitable duck foods. The benefits of this sort of management are two-fold: (1) loss of a mast crop does not eliminate all the food resources from a managed bottomland forest, and (2) ecological conditions are much improved for the remaining trees and they are more likely to produce an abundant crop of acorns. There are, however, two disadvantages: (1) regeneration of oaks is eliminted by both cultivation and winter flooding, and (2) plantings must be made annually and require repeated expenditures.

Fish Control. Carp are most destructive of aquatic plant life. They feed by rooting in the bottom soil and often destroy valuable duck food plants. Their feeding activities muddy the water, which inhibits the growth of submerged aquatics. Carp can be controlled by draining the marsh completely or by seining, but the surest method is by poisoning the water. If this method is used to remove carp, be sure you get advice from a conservation agent, or other professional, before proceeding.

Nesting. Breeding colonies of wood ducks can be developed in permanent marsh areas by installing nesting boxes of approved design. Raccoons are troublesome nest predators, but their depredations can be minimized. A leaflet with detailed instructions for building and installing artificial nest boxes for wood ducks can be obtained from the Conservation Departments of most states.

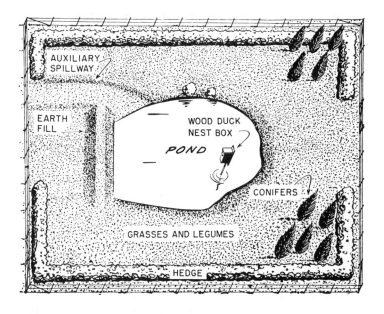

Planning & Construction of Marsh Area. In planning a duck marsh development, the advice of a competent agricultural engineer is essential. A clear understanding of the water supply, and how to impound or manipulate it, is necessary. An engineer can also provide a reasonable estimate of the cost of construction.

Before constructing a marsh area, the landowner should also check state laws governing the impoundment of water. Water rights laws should be clearly understood.

Perhaps the most important factor to consider when planning a duck marsh development project is water supply. Enough water must be available at the right times. Water can be stored in reservoirs, diverted from permanent or intermittent streams or ditches, or pumped from underground or surface supplies. But whatever the source, the supply should be adequate, dependable and of usable quality. When calculating water needs, allowance must be made for losses from evaporation, seepage and soak-in. If a storage reservoir is also managed for fish, enough water should be left after the peak use period to safeguard this resource.

The topography of the proposed marsh area should be fairly level. This will permit impoundment of water by low levees and allow efficient use of water. If the contour variations exceed 18 inches, additional leveeing should be considered.

Make certain that areas to be impounded have soils capable of holding water. Gravel or rock outcrops may permit excessive seepage and make it difficult to maintain water levels. Modest seepage in a reservoir often can be eliminated by sealing the bottom with bentonite.

Water control structures should be large enough to efficiently flood and drain managed units. They range from simple gated corrugated metal pipe to drop log, drop inlet, and radial gate structures of many designs modified to fit local conditions and needs. This is one of the things the engineer can help determine. Adequate provisions should also be made to accommodate excessive amounts of water. The design of emergency spillways depends on the expected extent and frequency of overflow.

Duck Mortality. Ducks are highly adaptable. If conditions in one location are unfavorable, they are willing and able to go elsewhere. They are not susceptible to many poultry diseases, but their lives are not exactly free of problems either.

In addition to nest losses, which are high, a large proportion of all ducklings hatched will fail to survive to flight time. Predators, such as mink and turtles and pike, will take their toll; so will floods and drought and hail. Ducks that leave the breeding ground will be exposed to hunting for more than four months, and the shotgun will claim nearly two-thirds of them. The remaining birds must survive lead poisoning, which each year accounts for one bird in twenty; botulism, which varies in importance from year to year but can be locally severe; and other diseases including fowl cholera and aspergillosis. Parasites of various kinds often weaken and sometimes kill ducks, but these tough birds have learned to live with most of them. Industrial pollution, especially the oils, sometimes takes an enormous toll. The birds are killed by poisoning or, more commonly, by exposure after being coated with this foul material.

Hunting is the most important mortality factor for most species of ducks and also is the most practical one for managers to influence. By carefully regulating the harvest, enough ducks can survive pike, droughts, disease and pollution, plus the shotgun, to perpetuate this marvelous resource.

Mallard Propagation

As mentioned earlier in this chapter, the mallard is the king of sport ducks in the United States and Canada. Most game bird raisers and waterfowl hunters value mallards above all other ducks, both for sport and table use. Their strong flight and natural wariness provide a test of skill for the hunter and they are quite adaptable and easy to rear for the game bird raiser.

Description: The Wild Mallard (Anas platyrhynchos platyrhynchos L.) The green head and white collar are distinguishing marks of the drake mallard in fall, winter and spring. A chestnut vest and curled black feathers over a white tail add to the handsome appearance. The drake shares with his comparatively drab mate a speculum (wing marking) of dark violet, edged front and back with narrow black bars which in turn are edged in white. Otherwise, the hen is buff or light brown marked and streaked with darker brown while the cheeks, throat and underparts are lighter. The feet of the drake are reddish orange but those of the hen and immature birds are paler yellowish-orange. The bill of the male is greenish yellow, whereas that of the female is usually orange with black splotches. In most areas adult males lose their bright breeding plumage by the end of July and in their eclipse plumage resemble the females. By late October most adult drakes have progressed into their next molt and are again easily identified from females. Young drakes are usually about a month behind the adult drake in completing the feather replacement. Average weights in fall range from two pounds eight ounces for immature females to three pounds for adult males.

Nesting and Brood Rearing. Mallards use many kinds of vegetation for nesting although they prefer fairly dry sites with rather tall vegetation. Tall upland weeds, dry marshes and hay fields are common nesting sites. Undisturbed grasses, lightly grazed pastures, and lightly flooded grass and sedges are also used but to a lesser degree.

The number of eggs in a mallard nest averages about ten or eleven in the first nesting attempt. If the nest is destroyed, a second clutch may be laid and this may contain fewer eggs. The incubation period is generally twenty-six to twenty-eight days. The ducklings appear fully feathered in about seven weeks and are generally able to start flying at fifty-two to sixty days of age.

Foods and Feeding Habits. The mallard is a surface feeder and is commonly observed "tipping up" to feed in shallow water. Medium to large marshes and marshy shorelines of lakes seem to be preferred. The mallard also feeds on dry land where corn, wheat, barley and acorns are favorite staples. Stubble fields are heavily used during the spring and fall. Sometimes they congregate on swathed grain fields near fall concentration centers and cause considerable loss of grain. In fall, vegetable matter comprises a high percent of the mallard's diet. In the newly hatched young, insects and other animal matter are important foods. As the duckling reaches the flying stage, more and more vegetable matter is eaten. The mallard is like other ducks in that it will feed on the foods most available.

The Domesticated Mallard. The wild mallard is the ancestor of most breeds of domestic ducks. Breeds such as the Pekin, Rouen, Cayuga, Indian Runner and Gray Call all originated from the mallard. An exception is the domestic Muscovy duck. It was developed from the wild Muscovy duck which is native to Mexico, Central America and South America.

The domestic breeds such as the Pekin and Rouen, which originated from the wild mallard, are generally easily recognized as distinct breeds by their characteristics. There is, however, considerable variation in the "wild mallards" kept by game breeders. These differences are not always easily recognized and they represent varying degrees of departure from the true wild bird, even though most of them are capable of some flight. These domestic mallards may differ from true wild birds in size, posture, facial markings, bill size and shape, egg size and shape, egg laying capacity, markings of young, and probably most important "behavior" or degree of innate wildness. The near wild mallard can be expected to lay only twenty to thirty eggs per year in captivity.

The true wild mallard has a long narrow bill. Its posture is quite horizontal and in general it has a trim, streamlined appearance. The downy young have a single line running across the face and this line can be recognized on the face of fully grown females even though it is not as distinct as in the downy young. Some domestic strains have two lines across the face. Some game breeders are acutely aware of the variation in strains of wild mallards kept in captivity and have developed good wild type birds.

In recent years, many raisers of game birds have propagated mallards. If these birds are to be released into open areas, certain things are important if the birds are to survive. Two important considerations are believed to be (1) a good wild strain of mallard must be used and (2) the ducklings must be reared and released in such manner that they will readily learn to live in the wild much as native wild birds. This was explained in greater detail in the chapters on raising upland game birds.

Raising And Releasing Mallard Ducklings

Starting Day Old Ducklings. It is important for game bird raisers who rear day old ducklings to prepare in advance for the arrival of their ducklings. In most cases these ducklings will be shipped parcel post when they are a day or two old. A brooder arrangement should be set up ready to receive ducklings, since they must be kept warm and dry and must be able to start taking food and water immediately. Any of several types of brooders used for domestic ducklings or other fowl will probably prove satisfactory. As was true for pheasants and other game birds, sanitation is very important and the brooder, the brooder house floor, the waterers and the feeders should all be clean and should be kept clean after the ducklings are received.

Whatever type of brooder is used it should be adjusted so the temperature at the level of the ducklings is from ninety degrees to ninety-five degrees F. A satisfactory brooder consists of a cluster of heat lamps (usually four) which are suspended approximately eighteen inches above the litter of the pen. Wood shavings or ground corn cobs make a good litter. A brooder guard encircles the area around the heat lamp cluster and keeps the ducklings from straying away.

Chick waterers which attach to a common fruit jar are placed within the brooder guard but not too close to the area warmed by the heat lamps. Lukewarm water should be used for the first few days. It is well to place the waterers on squares of cardboard so they will set level.

A supply of game bird starter mash should be obtained in advance. A local feed dealer can order this or he may recommend some substitute such as a turkey starter mash. Depending upon the number of ducklings, mash should be put in shallow pans which are placed conveniently within the brooder guard interspersed with the waterers. The pans should be sufficiently shallow so the food is readily available. The ducklings now have all the essentials of life—food, water and heat. In a day or two they will be taking food and water readily and the brooder guard can be removed allowing them to range about the brooder house. The food can be put into feeders which prevent wastage and larger waterers can be used.

Care After the Ducklings are Started. If the weather is warm and fair the ducklings can be allowed to range out of the brooder house when a few days old. If the house has a small exit or opening a circle of one inch woven wire can be constructed on the outside so the ducklings can come out and sun themselves but cannot stray away. A waterer and feeder can be put outside in this pen during the day. The ducklings should be put in at night and should be left in on days when the weather is cold and wet.

When ducklings are about two weeks old they will probably make little use of the brooder except at night and the heat lamps can be raised to about three feet above the brooder room floor.

At three weeks the ducklings can be moved to an open pen. There should be plenty of shade and some form of a shelter may be desirable in case of a storm. If there is no natural pond in this pen it is well to put in large pans of water so the ducklings can bathe and oil their feathers. At this time the local feed dealer may advise switching the food to a game bird grower mash.

Some propagators have supplemented the food supply after the ducklings are outside by suspending a light bulb about a foot over a pan of water. On warm summer nights many insects swarm around the light and many fall into the water. Ducklings will be active through much of the night catching and eating insects as they circle the light or fall into the pan of water. This arrangement has merit since the ducklings learn to eat some of the natural foods they will have to depend on when released into the wild.

Lettuce leaves are often available from grocery stores without cost and are relished by ducklings. Also, after the ducklings are at this age, it is advisable to collect some duckweed and other natural foods from nearby ponds daily to place in a large flat pan in the duck pen. This will help them develop a taste for the natural foods which they must live on when released. An ideal arrangement is where the holding pen contains a small natural pond where the ducklings can supplement their diet with natural foods.

It is exceedingly important that during the rearing process the ducklings be given as much seclusion and privacy as possible. **Do not make pets of them.** This one feature can defeat the entire program. Their contact with people should be limited only to the necessary functions of feeding, watering and cleaning the pens. Ducklings intended for release should be treated in such a manner as to keep them shy and wary, to retain all the wild instinct and characteristics that is possible.

A Second Method of Starting the Ducklings. In cases where small numbers of ducklings are to be started it may be impractical to buy heat lamps or other expensive brooder equipment. The method explained here has been used successfully to start fifteen or fewer ducklings. It consists of a cardboard box at least twenty-four by thirty inches in size into which is suspended an ordinary light bulb. A piece of burlap sack can be cut to fit into the bottom of the box or dry litter such as ground corn cobs can be used. Whatever is used, burlap or litter, it should be changed daily to keep the box dry and clean. The light bulb should be suspended so it is about twelve to fifteen inches from the bottom of the box. It should not be near the sides of the box since this may cause a fire. Also, in this connection it is well to attach the bulb and cord securely so it does not come loose and drop to the bottom of the box. The heat can be adjusted by covering the part of the top of the box over the bulb with a piece of cardboard. A sixty or seventy-five watt bulb should be satisfactory and the temperature should be about ninety degrees F. on the floor of the box below the bulb. An ordinary fruit jar chick waterer is adequate and food can be put in jar caps or other such containers.

While this method has proved satisfactory for starting ducklings, there is danger that too much attention will be given the ducklings. Do not make pets out of them, which in turn will detract from their suitability for release into the   wild. Every effort should be made to avoid this by not handling the ducklings and tending them only when necessary. As soon as the ducklings are well started they should be moved to facilities in a shed or outdoor pen as described earlier.

Releasing the Ducklings. The place where the ducklings are to be released should be selected well in advance of the time for the actual release. It is essential that the release be made on an isolated marsh area far away from human habitation, such as boat landings or camping areas. Many state owned wetlands will provide suitable habitat. The marsh selected should be of a reasonably large size and should contain a good interspersion of open water and clumps of emergent plants such as bulrushes, cattails or sedges.

It is recommended that game bird raisers release the ducklings on their own farm whenever suitable habitat is available. A good release age is thirty-five to forty days. The release should be made in the morning to allow maximum daylight hours in which to get accustomed to their new home. A day should be selected when the weather is warm and sunny. On the morning of the release the ducklings should be fed and watered and put in crates in which they are not overcrowded. It is recommended that the ducklings be released in groups of about twenty at one location. They should be released within two hours after being put into the crates. After release, further contact with people should be avoided in order to make them completely dependent on natural foods and to develop wildness. Do not attempt to feed them in the open after release as this will only tend to make the birds dependent on humans as a source of food.

Maintaining .Your Own Breeding Flock. The preceding information dealt largely with individuals raising day old ducklings supplied by a hatchery. Another method is for individuals to maintain their own flock of breeders and produce their own ducklings to be released according to the procedures which were described. If this second procedure is to be used the following information should be helpful.

Establishing a Captive Breeding Flock. The great importance of starting with and maintaining good quality breeding stock has already been discussed. It is advised that wild drakes be obtained under your state permit to sire a breeding flock. Ideally the holding pen should include both land and water in equal amounts and be completely covered. The fench should be about six feet high and of one inch mesh wire or it may have one inch mesh up about two or three feet and a two inch mesh wire above. Of course, each situation is different. If the pen cannot be covered the ducks will have to be kept wing clipped, as with pheasants. Also, if a natural source of water is not available tanks may have to be improvised to supply water for the ducks to drink and swim in. It may be necessary to practice predator control in the vicinity of the breeding pen. The pen should contain a building or other shelter for protection in winter. Usually a ratio of one drake for from three to six hens is satisfactory. The feed should be put in self-feeder type hopper spaced about the holding pen. Nest sites or shelters should also be placed about the breeding pens to provide a place for the hens to lay. A wooden box turned upside down and with a hole in one end makes a good laying site.

Fortunately some of our nationally known producers of feed make good foods for ducks. Specific information on feeds can be obtained from feed store operators or directly from the companies. Usually a prepared game bird food is fed along with some of the common small grains. About four weeks before eggs are to be saved for hatching, a game bird laying mash should be included as a major part of the diet. Grit such as gravel or granite should be supplied and it is also desirable to put out oyster shell during the laying season.

Handling and Incubating the Eggs. Duck eggs are best stored at forty-five to fifty-five degrees Fahrenheit and about sixty percent humidity. The eggs should not be held over ten days before setting in the incubator and they should be turned at least once a day while in storage. Certain models of incubators are made especially for incubation of goose and other waterfowl eggs and it is advisable to use one of these if possible. The manufacturer's instructions should be followed. Usually, forced draft incubators are operated from 99½° to 99¾° Fahrenheit. The humidity is often held at ninety percent until hatching time and then raised to ninety-four percent. Proper ventilation of the incubator is important. The eggs should be turned at least three times a day and a complete turn is desirable. Some operators find that sprinkling the eggs with water each day improves the hatch. The incubation period is usually about twenty-six to twenty-eight days. The manufacturer's instructions for fumigation, sanitation and general operation of the incubator should be followed. A basement room with a temperature from sixty to seventy degrees is a good location for the incubator. Eggs should always be gathered each day for best results.

Broody hens may be used to hatch ducks and geese much as discussed for pheasants but, due to problems involved, the practice is not generally recommended for game farmers.

Game Bird Permits

In most regions of the United States, a game farm license and federal propagation permit are required to keep pure wild type of Mallard. This rule also is true for raising pheasants, quail, geese, and other game birds. Usually the federal permit must be obtained before the game farm license will be issued. The cost of the permit and license isn't high but obtaining them is a detail that must be attended to. A local conservation agent will be able to supply the addresses where they can be obtained.

Raising Canada Or Other Geese

The Canada Goose is a very adaptable game bird to raise. It is not easy to raise them in captivity, however, for release into open hunting areas. The reason is that they are quick to become "pets" and become dependent on man for food and shelter. They may readily leave the captive area in later life but their chances for survival seem to be much less than for other game birds.

In raising geese of this or other type you must have some source of water but the area does not need to be extensive. Have as much water as possible available since geese must have water for breeding and copulation. However, a small pond three by four feet and six inches deep will be sufficient to raise a few birds. In addition to water, about three-quarters of your area should be land. This land area must have good grazing plants and should be of sufficient size to keep some grass coming up as the geese keep mowing it down. Geese are very intensive grazers and utilize this forage as a major source of food. Since they pull up sprouts of grass by the roots you must have a large area to allow for regrowth. In addition to grass, they should be fed small grain and poultry feed specifically formulated or recommended for geese. In winter, scraps of green lettuce and cabbage discarded by a grocery store can be very helpful if you can obtain it. Also in winter, second or third cutting, green leafy hay will help give the forage they need. Another item for raising geese is the huge amounts of gravel or grit they will consume. Two or three geese will use at least a pail of gravel each month. This is necessary for digestion (food grinding) in the gizzard.

Sex Determination. In propagating your own flock of geese, you must start with a pair—a goose and a gander. Since there is no easily observed coloring or other way of distinguishing between the two sexes, a manual sexing process must be used to be sure you have a bird of each sex. One of the most convenient ways of distinguishing between the sexes of geese and other game birds, is for the game bird raiser to sit in a well lighted location and then place the specimen upside down on his lap with the head of the bird hanging down between his legs and the tail pointed away from him. The feathers are then parted near the base of the tail in order to expose the vent to view. Next, endeavor to dialate the vent by pressing downward and outwardly with the thumbs on either side of the vent. Particularly, lean toward the front, pressing the tail backward with the other fingers of both hands at the same time the thumbs are spreading the clocca to facilitate the process of revealing the genital organs. The bird may resist by contracting its genital muscles but by applying gentle and firm steady pressure the goose will eventually relax and the sex organs will protrude, especially in the case of the gander where the penis will extend outward. If a female, the sex organ will appear as a round raised area like a shiny pimple or boil. The female's vent is usually wider and redder, whereas the male's is narrower, firmer and somewhat raised. An excellent time to vent-sex young waterfowl is just before they start to grow their flight feathers at which time the birds are easier to handle and sex than later when they are completely feathered out. Once you have determined sex, mark them with a colored leg band.

Most people who raise geese as game birds buy a pair or two, provide the proper environment and then let nature take its course. Good range is provided, some supplementary grain is fed, the wings are clipped or pinioned, and the geese are left on their own. In this semi-wild state the geese function as nature intended and gradually the flock increases.

Artifical Incubation. Artificial incubation of goose eggs has many of the same rules as for ducks, pheasants, quail, and other game birds. The process isn't generally recomemnded for beginners because of the equipment and skills required. If it is done, the raiser must be willing to follow a number of management "rules." Summarized, they include:

(1.) A good incubator must be secured which will provide the proper humidity and temperature at all times. It is recommended that an incubator especially made for geese eggs be used and the manufacturer's instructions followed carefully.

(2.) The incubator should be carefully fumigated before using. Fumigating materials can usually be secured through a poultry supply house in your area.

(3.) As with other game bird eggs, eggs for hatching must be carefully handled and stored.

Pinioning Geese. Wild geese must be pinioned so they can't fly away. The easiest way requires a pair of dull tin shears to cut off the ends of the wings at the proper place. Cut along the area shown in the following diagram, sprinkle before and after with a dry antiseptic powder, and check to be sure there is no excessive bleeding.

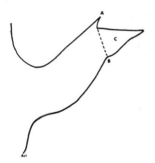

Diagrammatic view of goose wing. A is false wing. To pinion geese, after using antiseptic powder, cut along dotted line B with dull tin shears to cut off the end of one wing. C shows the removed portion.

Another method used by some allows the full wing to remain intact. This method, however, is more complicated and needs some skill to perform. It is done by tentomy which in effect drains the fluid from the wing joint which has the same results as a stiff leg from a knee injury. This method is permanent pinioning and can be performed on adult birds if necessary.

In other practices, geese can be managed much like other game birds. They are reasonably hardy and should thrive in small flocks if given proper care.

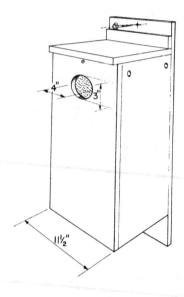

A Wood Duck House. Easy to build. Erect in a wet marsh by attaching to a sturdy pole set 4 to 6' above the high water level. May also be placed in trees up to 500 yards from a suitable water area.

Because of their similarities and need for water, ducks and geese might be raised together in the same area. Their management isn't exactly alike, but since their environment needs are similar it may be possible to raise them on one game farm.

Chapter VI

DEVELOPING A GAME BIRD
PRESERVE

As natural habitat becomes more scarce, the need for game preserves will increase. For hunters who may drive miles not knowing if they will see a bird, the game preserve offers a sure chance to shoot. Another use for game bird preserves is to give people the opportunity to tramp through the woods with, perhaps, only a camera in hand. This is becoming more and more popular as a relaxing and enjoyable way to spend a weekend or vacation as our urban sprawl continues and people work in more crowded and noise filled areas. Just sitting in a blind by the side of a pond on a cool fall day and watching the ducks fly will make a preserve seem worth the cost.

Preserve Areas

Abandoned submarginal farms make excellent areas for game bird preserves. Preferably, they should contain lakes, bogs, forest, grass lands, and fields which can be cropped for corn or other small grains to provide feed. Although most game preserves are a legal unit with fenced or posted boundaries, some are simply natural coverts not easily accessible to man and policed by nature. They may be remote tablelands far from roads, dense swamps, tracts of virgin forest, or open range where game is protected by sheer space. Many of our state and federal preserves are such areas. Preserves to serve as refuges for small birds may even be heavy cover within city limits where shooting is prohibited.

The shooting preserve must be kept as natural as possible. It should not become a "country club", but an area to serve real hunters.

Use Of Preserves

Preserves may be opened to the public or established as private hunting clubs with limited memberships sold. They can be commercial enterprises for a group or can be operated only for one person. In commercial preserves hunting dogs can be kept in a managed kennel with a fulltime trainer as a subsidiary enterprise. Dogs owned by hunters can be boarded and trained and others "rented" to members on a daily fee basis. Availability of trained dogs increases hunter success and greatly reduces the number of unrecovered cripples. Many preserves require hunters to use trained dogs.

Preserves Governed By State Rules And Regulations

Before starting a game preserve, write to your state Department of Wildlife and Conservation (or department with a similar name) which is usually located in your state capital. Ask for the rules and regulations governing private and commercially operated game preserves in your state. Laws vary a great deal, but most states allow a four to six month open hunting season in such areas. There are a few states, however, where preserves still are not legal. Most states require a preserve license.

Factors To Consider Before Starting A Game Bird Preserve

There are five basic factors that control the extent of game bird propagation for a given area:

1. The kind of land area available and how well the desired game birds can adapt to it.

2. The quality, quantity and distribution of available cover for game birds.

3. The distribution and abundance of game birds already on the land.

4. The presence of predators that prey on game birds.

5. Foods available for game birds (wild plants, small grains, etc.).

Read all the information you can about game preserves. All of the earlier chapters in this book, especially the first one on propagating game birds in open areas, will be helpful. If possible, visit several preserves in your area, both public and private, and get as much information from the managers as possible.

Also, carefully consider the cost of establishing a game preserve. Figure the cost of building brooding facilities if used, growing and flight pens, dog kennels, a duck flight tower, and lodging facilities. Include the cost of buying or leasing land, raising the number of birds needed, and advertising your preserve to get customers. Figure the cost of labor, equipment, and other operating expenses, such as recovery loss. On a well-operated preserve, a recovery rate of seventy to eighty percent of the birds released can be expected. From these facts you can establish the amount of return to be expected from your original investment. Be sure you have enough operating capital. A sample budget for a small game bird preserve is given below. It is for a proposed shooting preserve and based mainly on recommendations of the Wisconsin Soil Conservation Service and findings from a study of privately owned game preserves in Wisconsin during 1966.

Proposed Budget, 400-Acre Preserve, Harvesting 6,000 Pheasants With A $55,000 Investment

Annual Costs:

Cost of birds (8,000 pheasants 12-weeks old)
at $1.75 per bird $14,000
Non-family labor at $1.75 per hour, 2,100 hours 3,675
Feeding—until release 1,200
Establishment of 35 acres of crops or shooting
fields at $17 per acre 595

Establishment of 75 acres of grass and legumes (annual cost with a 10-year amortization)	300
8 acres of shrub planting (annual cost with a 10-year amortization)	30
Utilities	200
Insurance	250
Advertising	400
Taxes	600
Supplies and equipment	500
Maintenance	500
Miscellaneous	200
TOTAL ANNUAL COSTS	$22,450
Annual income (6,000 pheasants at $5.50)	$33,000
Net income (income minus costs)	10,550
Depreciation	540
Interest on capital (6%)	3,300
Return to family labor and management	$ 6,710

Cost and income figures may vary in other areas but this budget may serve as a valuable guide for developing your own.

After reviewing the costs, if you decide to operate a game preserve, pick a good location. If it is to be commercially operated, it should be in an area which can provide a large number of potential customers who have the time and money to hunt. The terrain and cover should be similar to natural hunting conditions in the area. Build facilities needed to handle the birds, dogs, and customers. Then lay out good shooting areas and plant the recommended cover crops.

The size of the preserve should depend upon its use. If you plan to produce birds for sale, to be released in other regions, the farm can be relatively small. In contrast, commercial or private hunting preserves are usually large—1,000 acres or more.

Game Bird Stocking

Game bird stocking is man's effort to increase game supply on a range by obtaining game elsewhere and releasing it on that range. Whether to stock or not depends on many factors. It is most practiced in one of the following situations:

1. When a good game bird habitat has been depopulated by severe weather or other temporary factor.
2. When such a habitat is suitable for a game bird species that does not exist there, or near there.
3. When a small game bird preserve is heavily stocked and heavily hunted shortly after stocking.

In reality, nature herself normally stocks her game ranges. Help from man may be necessary when one of the above conditions exist.

Management Practices

The most basic and important game bird preserve management practice is habitat preservation, or if necessary, restoration. Small game bird habitat is the complex of soil, water, and plants—commonly called "cover"—in which small game birds exist. It is a "life range" that must include escape cover, winter cover, food and water, cover to rear young birds, and even cover to play. A lack of one or more of these requirements must be corrected if an area is to support game in harvestable numbers.

Condition of the soil and its plant covering is the most important determining factor in small game bird yield for any area. Game habitat is dynamic. Cover conditions are constantly changing. These changes influence the quantity and distribution of game birds. The most important of these changes is plant succession, as demonstrated by the evolution of grassy fields into brushland. Good small game bird management attempts to direct plant succession in the right time and place. Planting food crops like small grain, fencing, and fire protection advance the plant succession; cows, the axe, plowing, and fire can reverse it.

Habitat restoration isn't a simple and quick process. Programs may require five years or more to produce marked increases in the number of game birds.

Once cover is established, it must be managed. Heavy cover is necessary to keep birds confined to the release site. In hunting preserves, game birds are usually released a short time before the hunt. Because of this, suitable cover is essential to prevent wide dispersement. Some cover plants recommended are sudan grass, sorghum, corn, millets, switchgrass, Reed canary-grass, and Sericea Lespedeza. They should not be planted in wide rows so that birds have unlimited running space. Cover crops should serve a twofold purpose: to promote conservation of soil and other natural resources, and to assist in achieving preserve objectives, including sound bird management. Planting should be done to protect against erosion and other useless vegetation. The following guidelines are recommended for planting and caring for cover crops and shrubbery:

1. Combinations of cover plants are better than single species.
2. In fall, thirty to fifty-foot strips should be mowed at one hundred to two hundred foot intervals.
3. Generally cover release areas should be fifty to sixty feet wide and one hundred to two hundred feet long.
4. Shrub plantings may be made to reduce the size of the field and to screen unsightly areas. Such plantings are also useful for release of birds late in the season. Recommended shrubs include ninebark, Tartarian, honeysuckle, Russian Olive, redosier, and silky dogwood. Other species adapted to a particular area are also acceptable.
5. A meadow border is recommended around the cover release area. This will involve a substantial portion of the preserve and can be harvested for hay. A grass-legume mixture is recommended for such an area.

Trespassing and vandalism may be a problem but most preserve operators don't feel that they are serious. Preserve operators in Wisconsin felt that fixed costs of a preserve—such as taxes and insurance, particularly liability insurance—were very high. Their concern was more about insurance than taxes.

In summary, whether or not you maintain a successful and economical game bird preserve probably will depend upon the following factors:

1. Size and type of area that is available.
2. Use now being made of the land.
3. Character of the land.
4. Accessibility.
5. Kind of game birds propagated.
6. Facilities made available for visiting sportsmen.

7. Amount of work you do.

8. Amount of capital you have available for investment.

9. Organization and management practices conducted.

10. State and federal game laws.

A well-developed and managed preserve can become a good source of income and a pleasure to own and operate.

Country Chuckles, Cracks & Knee-Slappers

Edited by Mike Lessiter

"We borrowed my sister-in-law's copy of More Country Chuckles. We laughed so hard, I think it would make a great gift."
—Jacob Beyerl, Colby, Wis.

Get set for a wild and crazy, laugh-a-minute ride down the back roads of America. This 256-page book's 46 giggle-inducing chapters will knock you off your rocker with 1,241 of the best gut-busting jokes you'll find anywhere.

256 pages..........................$11.95

Plus shipping and handling. See ordering information below.

More Country Chuckles, Cracks & Knee Slappers

Edited by Sandra Lessiter

"I find the humor in both Country Chuckles and More Country Chuckles touching the funny bone."
—Walter Scholz, Canada

When you recover from reading our first book of country humor, *Country Chuckles, Cracks And Knee-Slappers,* our 208-page second volume of country humor will set your sides aching all over again! These new jokes in the same flavor of our highly popular first book are funny enough to put you on the floor and clean enough to tell the pastor! If you enjoyed the first book, you'll love this one!

208 pages $12.95

Plus shipping and handling. See ordering information below.

ORDERING INFORMATION:
Send your check or credit card information to:
Lessiter Publications, P.O. Box 624, Brookfield, WI 53008-0624

FOR FASTER SERVICE:
Call: (800) 645-8455 (U.S. only) **or** (262) 782-4480 • **Fax:** (262) 782-1252
E-mail: info@lesspub.com • **Web site:** www.lesspub.com

Add $4.00 for shipping and handling for the 1st book and $1 shipping and handling for each additional book. Wisconsin residents need to add 5.1 percent sales tax. For foreign and Canadian shipping, add $8.00 for the first book and $5.00 for each additional book purchased. Payable in U.S. funds drawn on a U.S. bank only.